SHERRILL CANET

A LA CARTE

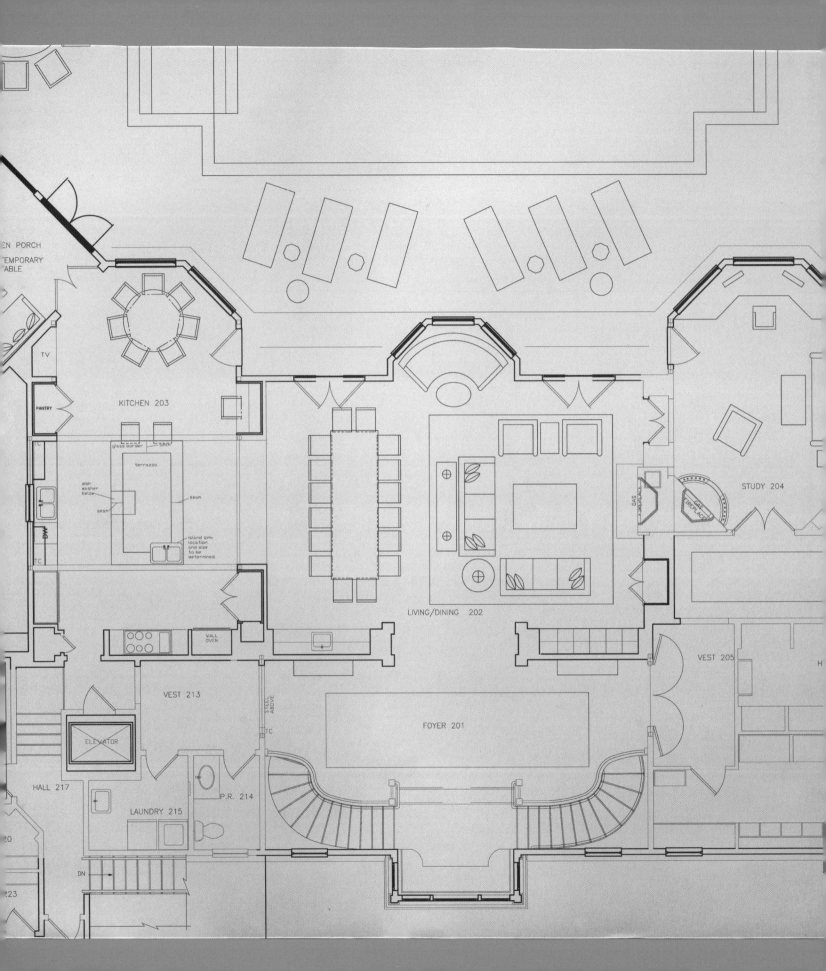

EN PORCH

EMPORARY
ABLE

TV

PANTRY

KITCHEN 203

glass border   seam

terrazzo

dish
washer
below   seam

seam

island sink
location
and size
to be
determined

TC

TC

DW

WALL
OVEN

STEEL
ABOVE

TC

LIVING/DINING 202

STUDY 204

GAS
FIREPLACE

GAS
FIREPLACE

VEST 205

VEST 213

ELEVATOR

HALL 217

P.R. 214

FOYER 201

LAUNDRY 215

DN

23

SHERRILL CANET

A LA CARTE

THE ELEMENTS OF AN ELEGANT HOME

PRINCIPAL PHOTOGRAPHY BY

MICHEL ARNAUD

EDITORIAL DIRECTOR: SUZANNE SLESIN

DESIGN: STAFFORD CLIFF

PRODUCTION: DOMINICK J. SANTISE, JR.

TEXT: DAMARIS COLHOUN

POINTED LEAF PRESS, LLC.

CONTENTS

As a second-grader in Franklin Lakes, New Jersey, Sherrill was athletic, studied the piano, and played house.

Sherrill started modeling when she was fourteen years old. Three years later, she sat for a head shot to audition for a television commercial.

OPPOSITE A contact sheet of different poses was taken while on a photography shoot for Harper's Bazaar when Sherrill was eighteen years old.

THIS PAGE After graduating from high school, Sherrill pursued a career as a model while studying at Fordham University in New York. During the following four years she also traveled between New York and Paris, Milan, Hamburg, and London, where this photograph was taken for Harvey Nichols, the London department store. It was published in an English magazine in 1979.

A FLAIR FOR EXPERIMENTAL, RULE-BREAKING DESIGN

For the past twenty years, Sherrill Canet's career as an interior designer has struck a balance between two seemingly opposite styles. On the one hand are her passions for historical decorating, European antiques and the Gilded Age mansions that checker the North Shore of Long Island, where she now lives. On the other hand is her flair for experimental, rule-breaking design, kindled by a creative energy that is self-confident, curious, and resourceful. "Great Gold Coast homes and a personal passion for English and French antiques have definitely molded my sensibility," Sherrill says. "My challenge is to create interiors that take those Old World things and make them fresh again."

Sherrill's first love—and the touchstone for her most classical decorating style—were antiques from the eighteenth and nineteenth centuries, a passion first cultivated while living in London with her husband, Eduardo. "I had a specific focus at first," Sherrill explains. "Mainly English, French, and Italian antiques, but I was attracted to anything unusual, like exceptionally carved or finely painted pieces, or a design made from an unusual wood." A hobby of locating small, special dealers became an obsession, and after studying design at the Inchbald School in London, Sherrill moved back to New York, where she opened her first antiques shop, in Locust Valley, Long Island, and then a second one, on Third Avenue and 62d Street, on Manhattan's Upper East Side. "I shopped incessantly," Sherrill says. "My frame of reference was always personal. I felt that if I was drawn to a piece, then somebody else would like it too."

As a side business to her antiques shops, Sherrill began designing interiors for her customers. Before long, Sherrill was buying exclusively for clients whose homes she was decorating. And for every piece of furniture that went to a client, another found its way into Sherrill's house. "I would look at a beautiful object and, in a sense, try to re-create an authentic atmosphere around it that would make the piece feel fresh and new," Sherrill says.

In re-imagining these history-filled rooms, the stories of her own 1919 house and its neighboring estates and summer cottages—monuments to a bygone era of entertaining on a large scale and for an opulent lifestyle—were fodder for creative inspiration. She researched old decorating books about Gold Coast architecture, interiors, and gardens for clues on how to reinterpret the colors, furnishings, and textiles of the well-coordinated period rooms, all of which would become the foundation for her classical, elegant style.

As her clientele expanded, so did Sherrill's interests. She gave up her antiques stores and began to seek out designs from every period, including wonderful examples from the mid-twentieth century, and pieces from such far-flung locales as Italy, England, France, Scandinavia, Russia, and Asia. "If I saw something cool, unusual, and useful, I bought it," Sherrill says. Inspired by these eclectic objects, whether an eighteenth-century painted Italian chest of drawers or an Art Deco headboard—maybe as a special homage to Gatsby's legendary Long Island— Sherrill developed a more lighthearted approach to decorating. Combining these unusual objects from all over the world into romantic vignettes was a skill she credits to the styling experience she gained by arranging objects and furniture in her shops. "You can't just have a jumble of antiques in your window and on your sales floor," she says. "You have to create combinations of pieces that catch people's eye and grab hold of their imagination."

The same applies to decorating. "I want to capture someone's attention the second he or she walks into a room," she explains. "Then I want to hold the person's interest with out-of-the-ordinary pieces."

This eclectic approach to buying and styling marked a new phase in Sherrill's career, during which she developed a charming country style. "I love to work in the moment, and this style of design really speaks to that," Sherrill says. "It's rooted in traditional decorating, but there is always an unexpected twist to soften things up." That twist, according to Sherrill, is "anything that takes the seriousness out of the room—a sisal carpet, whimsical accessories, unusual finishes, or a wild splash of color," she explains. "It's about using contrast in a subtle way, pairing clean lines with sensuous ones, or mixing painted furniture with formal antiques. It's about trusting your eye and being willing to take more risks."

Although Sherrill's rooms reveal a sharp sense of historical rigor, she insists that her most traditional interiors retain elements of youthfulness and surprise. "You don't want to fall into the rut of period decorating," she says. "This style needs to be nurtured and kept alive with accessories and layerings of different levels of formality. For example, I like to apply historical colors in an unexpected way. Also, understand that these are not projects for which furnishings, fabrics, and carpets can be mail-ordered in one pop. I want my clients to become collectors."

Ten years after she first moved into the Long Island house, Sherrill had redecorated it from top to bottom, replacing the somewhat somber, old-fashioned textiles and furniture with lighter, more contemporary versions. But the designer recalls having to strike a deal with her husband, who was getting nervous about her passion for constant experimentation. "The library has always been his favorite room," she says. "I promised him I wouldn't ever change it drastically. And that promise has taught me to work within certain boundaries. Changing a room, or making it feel current through the years without overhauling it entirely, is an effective tool to have in your back pocket, especially if it's going to keep the man in the house happy."

Recently, Sherrill has been working in a more contemporary style, using clean-lined furniture and exotic materials. She now favors textures such as parchment, exotic woods, leathers, and hides.

"If the architecture of the home is traditional, as mine is, then the interior goes in the opposite direction. It's all about subverting tradition and using irony to make it look new. I love that back-and-forth," she adds. And, of course, how far backward or forward she goes depends entirely on her clients' needs. "I've lived in an Old World home. I've lived in a romantic, country home. And today, my home is as sharp and modern as it's ever been. I understand these styles from the inside out." Not one to set things in stone, Sherrill adds with a wink, "That said, I'll always find room to play."

OPPOSITE Sherrill was photographed in the living room of her Locust Valley, New York, home for a 2001 article in *Classic American Home*.

A TIMELESS MIX SPANNING HUNDREDS OF YEARS

The decorating practice of mixing furniture of different styles and periods and from different countries has been around for a long time. The great English country houses of the seventeenth and eighteenth centuries often contained Roman and Greek antiquities, French, English, Chinese, and Japanese furnishings, and decorative objects and paintings from England and the continent, commissioned or purchased, perhaps on the Continent when the gentleman-owner took his coming-of-age Grand Tour. As the house passed down through the ages, succeeding generations often added antiques and contemporary furnishings they purchased in England or abroad, putting their personal stamp on these grand interiors. A timeless mix spanning hundreds of years would be the end result, suited to the tastes of the current occupants. While Americans may not live in homes passed down by their great-grandparents, they nevertheless embrace a taste for interior decoration that is not tied to a specific time or place, preferring an eclectic look that seems to have been assembled over time, not put together overnight. The best designers, and certainly one can count Sherrill Canet in this group, have the ability to create environments that are both personal and warm, elegant yet relaxed, reflecting the needs and tastes of the people who live in them. My pleasure as an antiques dealer is being able to work with designers of Sherrill's and her clients' caliber. That is when I am able to share my passion for the wonderful furniture and decorative objects at Kentshire. There is no greater satisfaction than when a client responds to a piece, when they excitingly "get it," and begin to share our enthusiasm for its uniqueness. Great designers always try to buy the best for their clients, yet the best doesn't have to mean the most expensive. Many of the best things were made by anonymous artisans of the past—craftspeople who injected their souls into the things they created. At Kentshire, we try to buy only things that appeal to us on an emotional level as well as a practical one—objects where the design, craftsmanship and quality of materials make them memorable. Of course, it's always necessary to be sure the piece is authentic, that it is what it's purported to be, and that the quality of the workmanship and the materials are of the highest standard. Provenance, too, is important, and certainly adds value, but it's the beauty of the object itself that is paramount. Kentshire is a family business, founded in 1940. Fred Imberman, my brother-in-law, and I have been here for the past forty years. Our wives, Marcie and Ellen, led us into the world of antique jewelry twenty-two years ago. And most recently, my niece, Carrie, and nephew, Matthew, have joined us. We look forward to a future of sharing our passion for the very best with our wonderfully loyal designers, clients, and new friends we meet along the way.

Robert Israel is a partner in Kentshire Galleries in New York.

OPPOSITE A pair of poufs covered in a leopard-print fabric from Old World Weavers is arranged near a nineteenth-century English Regency center table from Kentshire Galleries in New York. The limestone floor of the high-ceilinged room is inlaid with wood to create a strong, subtle graphic element.

A TIME OF UNPARALLELED ELEGANCE AND SPLENDOR

The North Shore of Long Island has always been a very special place for me. Since 1959, along with its trustees, I have dedicated myself to the preservation of Old Westbury Gardens, listed on the National Registry of Historic Places. Set on 160 rolling acres, Westbury House—a magnificent Charles II-style mansion that was the former country estate of my husband's uncle, financier and sportsman John S. Phipps (1874-1958), his wife, Margarita Grace Phipps, and their four children—is widely considered one of the most beautiful English-style country estates in North America.

Originally, the Phipps family properties consisted of five houses in Old Westbury. All of these houses were next to one another, making tea and dinner wonderful family times. In those days, life on the Gold Coast was filled with activities, including polo, foxhunting, tennis, golf, and sailing. Today, the North Shore is still filled with the many delights of that bygone era, which add to the sophisticated charm and appeal of the region. The sporting country life and numerous examples of its fine architecture continue to attract families to the area, keeping the traditions of the past alive.

Preserving the splendors of the past and respecting tradition while appreciating modern design and the conveniences of our time has been Sherrill Canet's design mission. She has an abiding interest in fine architecture and is committed to integrating the interior of the home with its landscape and surroundings. Combining a fine knowledge of antiques and a talent for incorporating them seamlessly into her projects, the traditional flavor of many of her interiors is not only maintained but celebrated. Traditional principles are respected, while a modern lifestyle with all of the amenities and luxuries that define comfort today bring her projects into the twenty-first century.

Mary S. Phipps, the chairman of Old Westbury Gardens, is a socially active figure in New York and Long Island, who contributes to many philanthropic causes.

OPPOSITE A romantic view looking north from the house offers a glimpse of Old Westbury Gardens that captures the enduring talents of George A. Crawley, the landscape designer who planned the estate at the beginning of the twentieth century.

CASTLE GUILD, LATE DANIEL GUGGENHEIM ESTATE, PORT WASHINGTON, LONG ISLAND, N. Y.

Res. of Mr. Geo. D. Pratt, Glen Cove, N. Y.

M18919

PREVIOUS PAGES In 1955, famed photographer Margaret Bourke-White took this aerial winter view of the Gold Coast, as the area on the North Shore of Long Island, New York, was known. Although many of the vast estates, with their large mansions that belonged to the wealthiest members of society, have disappeared—some torn down, some turned into public institutions—others have taken their place. New houses, many inspired by English country manors or French châteaux of the past, have been built, and the natural beauty, privacy, and proximity to New York City have contributed to the continued exclusivity of the area.

LEFT A postcard depicts the turreted, Kilkenny Castle–inspired Castle Gould, in Port Washington, New York, designed in the first decade of the twentieth century by Hunt and Hunt, one of New York's most prestigious architectural firms at the time. Built by Howard Gould, the financier son of railroad tycoon Jay Gould, the estate was later owned by the industrialist and philanthropist Daniel Guggenheim and his wife, Florence. The estate, now a museum and devoid of its elegant furnishings, is part of the Sands Point Preserve.

LEFT Built in 1913 and designed by the architectural firm of Trowbridge and Ackerman in an English Tudor style, Killenworth, as philanthropist George Dupont Pratt's house is called, once had grounds tended by fifty gardeners. Since the 1950s, it has been used as a retreat for Russian diplomats.

RIGHT Designed by Oliver Cope, this newly built Long Island house, with its walled garden, the New York architect explains, "takes its inspiration from multiple sources, but has strong overtones from French country houses. The steeply pitched tile roofs, the eaves broken by dormers, and the walls of limestone and pale brick are a nod to Normandy."

BELOW RIGHT Another house in the same overall palette, by the same architect, has a decidedly English Jacobean flair. "The connection between the house and its garden is central to the development of country houses," says Cope. "This house has multiple porches, terraces, and second-floor balconies that are each linked to a vista or a view of the garden. The house also illustrates the richness made possible by establishing a strong central symmetry that has been overlaid by asymmetries to create an underlying sense of order that is enriched with romanticism."

LEFT English-born Peter Cummin, whose firm, Cummin Associates, is based in Stonington, Connecticut, laid out the beautiful gardens on a Gold Coast estate to include a gazebo in a formal garden overlooking Long Island Sound, left, and a traditional vegetable and flower cutting garden, below left.

OPPOSITE An arched doorway leads from the walled garden, with its handmade bricks now covered in ivy, to the cobblestoned driveway by the front entrance of the house.

ABOVE Beautifully sited, the rear
garden of a new house by the firm
Oliver Cope Architect overlooks
Long Island Sound.

ABOVE For decades—this photograph
was taken in 1946—a spot with
exquisite views of Long Island Sound
has been the place for people residing
on the Gold Coast to relax and moor
their sailing boats.

My house was built in Locust Valley, New York, in 1919 as a summer cottage for Jackson E. Reynolds, a financier and president of the First National Bank. It was designed by Harrie Thomas Lindeberg, who had a reputation as a "gentleman architect" with a knack for historical but innovative country homes, in an era when hundreds of great estates made the North Shore—or, as it came to be known, the Gold Coast—a special, rarified place to live. Lindeberg had worked at McKim, Mead, and White, one of New York's premier architectural firms, and by the time this house was completed, was on his way to becoming one of the most successful architects of his day. While the façade made overtures to tradition, the grounds were keenly attuned to the leisure activities of the day. There was a barn, as well as a carriage house for motorcars, and with plenty of surrounding land—now long subdivided—the estate was designed to entertain the Reynolds family and their summer guests who, I imagine, enjoyed every pleasure the Gilded Age had to offer. With its classical columns, black-painted shutters, clapboard siding, and Colonial Georgian facade, the twenty-room house remains, even nearly a century after it was first built, true to the historical style of the area.

LEFT The imaginative ornamental metal screen door for the front entrance of the house—depicting a spider's cobweb with a butterfly and a fly in its lair— was designed by Lindeberg more than ninety years ago and is still in place.

OPPOSITE Set on a graceful rise, the clapboard house with classical detailing was once a summer residence and is now the Canet family's year-round home.

In the late 1980s, when we first moved in, the house was in great condition, and all the rooms had been meticulously maintained. As my personal style evolved and my family expanded, the house was slowly transformed. Furniture styles came and went; color palettes changed; and rooms were redecorated to accommodate our active, casual lifestyle—as when I turned a small, unused formal sitting room into a media room equipped to survive two rambunctious boys. We were lucky to find photographs of our house as it looked long before we came to live there. The transformations not only document the evolution of the way such interiors were lived in but reflect the changes in my decorating as it suited the shifting needs of my family. My hope is to introduce you to my personal style and to my firm belief that decorating your home is never a one-time event but, rather, an exciting process that develops over time.

LEFT Sherrill and Eduardo Canet were photographed with Alejandro, their second son, at the time they moved into the house. His older brother, Eduardo, was born in London seventeen months earlier.

OPPOSITE The original 1940 William Helburn edition of *Domestic Architecture of H.T. Lindeberg* is displayed on an eighteenth-century Italian armchair in the house. The book was reprinted by Acanthus Press in 2003.

1

MY HOME AS A DESIGN LABORATORY

STYLE SHEET 1: MY VERY OWN DESIGN LABORATORY

When it comes to designing interiors for my clients, my home is ground zero. For the last twenty years, I have subjected my Long Island home—a Georgian Colonial-style in Locust Valley, New York—to countless projects, makeovers, and mini-renovations, effectively transforming the traditional house, which I share with my husband and two sons, into a laboratory for design—minus the beakers and test tubes, of course. Filled with photographs that document my various experiments in style, this first chapter will take you on a photographic tour, from the day I moved in twenty years ago to today. The photographs, I hope, will give you an intimate sense of my personal development as a designer, and a taste of the three styles I am most expert in and passionate about: classical Old World elegance, gracious country charm, and contemporary tailored chic.

Our house was designed in 1919 by Harrie T. Lindeberg, left, a celebrated architect of the Gilded Age, who, at the time, was renowned for his modern interpretations of grand country homes and estates.

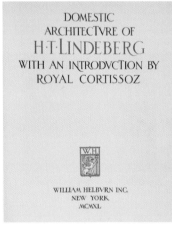

DOMESTIC
ARCHITECTVRE OF
H·T·LINDEBERG
WITH AN INTRODVCTION BY
ROYAL CORTISSOZ

W.H

WILLIAM HELBVRN INC.
NEW YORK
MCMXL

My husband and I moved into the house in 1988, when I was pregnant with my second son, Alejandro, shown top right, with his older brother, Eduardo. At the time, I owned two antiques shops, one in Locust Valley, New York, and another in New York City, above right center. My focus was primarily on seventeenth- and eighteenth-century English and French antiques, and anything else that I thought was fabulous and unusual.

Living in a traditional style home, amidst a revolving collection of furniture and objects from periods as diverse as Victorian England, French Regence, and eighteenth-century Italy, I took a very classical approach to my interiors, choosing Persian carpets, detailed window treatments, and formal textiles, like velvets, silk damasks, and brocades in rich colors like teal, burgundy, and gold, right.

I wanted to honor the history and the original millwork, moldings, and ironwork of the house with interiors that felt authentic, not pastiche-like, or sterile.

To keep the rooms feeling fresh, I brought in chinoiserie textiles and porcelains, above, as well a lively mix of European antiques and textured fabrics, and also included both casual and formal finishes—like faux crocodile and burnished leathers, below.

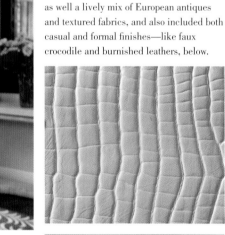

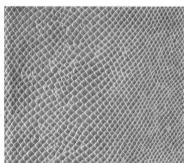

By the 1990s, I felt I knew this Old World, classical look inside and out. I needed a new challenge. My taste was beginning to change. I still craved a traditional style, but I wanted it to feel less serious.

I have always been inspired by the interiors of Sister Parish and Albert Hadley, above, both of whom had a knack for making traditional rooms feel fresh and contemporary. I shifted my buying focus to the nineteenth century, searching for cleaner-lined Directoire and Empire pieces, as well as painted furniture from Sweden, Italy, and France.

As the years went on, I started taking more risks, throwing rooms a curveball, by lacquering my dining rooms walls a brilliant Kelly green, left, or giving the old-fashioned architecture of my house a subversive wink. Seeing a dining room by the famous French firm of Jansen, below, I recreated my version of the trompe l'oeil trellis, below left.

The Linley console, below, was included in my debut collection of furniture for Stark. It can be custom-made in a variety of sizes and is available in numerous finishes. In its original version, it was covered in ivory faux-crocodile leather.

When I used antiques, I freshened them up with bright accessories, such as cobalt-blue glass, above, and kept surfaces unadorned. To create contrast, I became brasher, and I used bolder pieces to make strong statements.

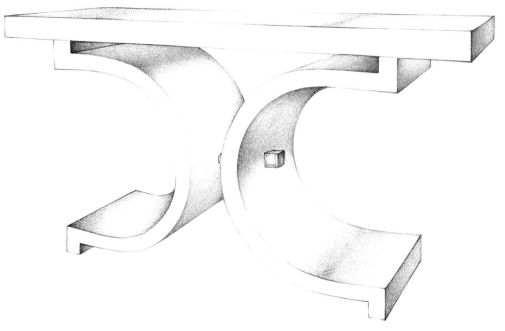

By the mid-2000s, I had sold my two shops and was designing collections of modern upholstered furniture, cabinets, and coffee tables for the Stark companies, many of which wound up in my house and, in some cases, replaced my antiques. I also began experimenting with a style that was out and out modern, inspired by twentieth century design styles like Hollywood Regency and French Moderne, as well as the work of such designers as Billy Baldwin, Karl Springer, and

Dorothy Draper. Details became tidier, too. Nail-head trims, upholstery piping, and a few select objects edged out swags, fringe, and distracting clutter. In a dramatic departure from my more traditional style, this smart, graphic look—rooted in contemporary design history—was an absolute counterpoint to the architecture of my house, and strayed far from the parameters its style typically demands. So, with no further ado, I welcome you to my home. I hope you enjoy the tour.

Walk through the front door of my home, and you'll find yourself in the foyer. It's an opportunity for first impressions, but it's also the main thoroughfare, leading people into the living room and up the stairwell. I always want it to be exciting and welcoming. After we had settled in and decorated the other rooms, I began designing the foyer with some considerations in mind: first, the traditional Georgian architecture of the house; second, the living room's extensive collection of eighteenth-century French and English antiques, acquired during our five years of living abroad; and last, the glamorous chandelier, a large vintage piece that probably once hung in a hotel. With these components in mind, I set about creating an entry hall that would have Old World panache. Since then, my foyer has undergone a number of metamorphoses. Although today it's rather contemporary, the basic functions of the furnishings have remained: a console or bench where I can toss my keys; a mirror and a pair of lamps, for subtle, warm lighting; and a few decorative objects. With wood floors, old-fashioned textiles, and antique furniture, the foyer has always made a literal connection to the classic exterior. Today, the space's modern palette and furnishings are more of a counterpoint to the architecture, updating it without abandoning it. Four images document the evolution of my foyer's personality over the course of twenty years. From strictly antique, to whimsical and eclectic, to sculptural and sleek, these dramatic transformations showcase the progression of my personal style. Eight years ago, I settled on the grand chandelier, and I'm still in love with it.

OPPOSITE In the beginning, the foyer's style was rooted in Victorian England: waxed wood floors, draperies made from vintage embroidered textiles that came from Turkish smoking rooms, Persian area rugs, and antique pillows. Accenting the creamy walls are muted strokes of red, navy, and gold. By the front door, a low bench and a carved, French gilt mirror indicated that this was the entry hall. Even though the palette was muted, drop-crystal, three-armed sconces with custom-made shades kept the hall bright and welcoming.

RIGHT A decade later, Paco, the Canets' boxer, posed in the foyer. The color palette was lightened to connect it more closely to that of the adjoining living room, which had just been redecorated. The floors were painted in a graphic diamond-parquet pattern. Gone are the Turkish tapestries and Persian carpets. In their place, Sherrill substituted embroidered draperies of pale blue-and-chocolate Bergamo linen that were, she says, "crisp and elegant." A pair of understated, clean-lined hurricane lamps replaced the fussier sconces.

By the early 1990s, I had replaced the foyer's once-Victorian and then quite exotic decor with eclectic objects for a lighter, more youthful look.

LEFT For a creamy, burnished look, the walls were finished in Venetian plaster to act as a suitable background for the gilded French console, the carved wood Dutch Colonial mirror, a pair of glass lamps from Italy, and an African dish on a stand.

OPPOSITE Today, the foyer with its cool gray walls has stepped into the twenty-first century. The sculptural Linley console—a white crocodile-leather piece Sherrill designed as part of a collection for Stark—holds an eighteenth-century statue of Quan Yin, the Buddhist goddess of compassion. Handblown glass lamps and a mercury glass vase update the antique cut-corner Dutch Colonial mirror.

While neither a foyer nor a stairway is the main event, both are highly trafficked areas that lead people from one place to the next all day long. So please, don't neglect them! To connect the two adjacent spaces, I coordinated their color palettes. Originally, I wanted to hang a beautiful painting in the stairway, but since I wasn't ready to buy a major piece of art at the time, I decided to frame a panel of wallpaper from Gracie, a New York firm that has specialized in hand-painted Chinese- and Japanese-style wallpapers since 1898. I originally bought the slate-blue and gray floral panel for a room I designed when I was invited for the first time to be in New York's prestigious Kips Bay Showhouse in 2003. I liked it so much I brought it home when the event was over.

LEFT An eighteenth-century bench, upholstered in lavish Bergamo velvet, makes the foyer feel distinctive. The custom Penn & Fletcher embroidery on the silk Bergamo pillow was specially designed to match the draperies' motif.

OPPOSITE The profile of Quan Yin is delineated against the stair, where the chocolate-colored runner is trimmed in an ivory band for a crisp look. The framed antique wallpaper fragment acts as a visual connection between the two floors and makes a dramatic impact. The antique crystal ball atop the newel post reflects the light, as do the sparkling rows of glass diamonds in the chandelier. Lupita sits at the top of the stairs.

The living room is the heart of my home, and when I'm in the mood to experiment with a new style, it's where I start tinkering. When a look sticks, everything else in the home follows suit. My first go-round with the living room was inspired by my passion for antiques, which I was buying at the time for my shops. My frame of reference for stocking my antiques stores was that if I wanted a piece for myself, it would no doubt sell in the store. That allowed me to shop with abandon and enjoy each object for a time.

LEFT In the early 1990s, Sherrill painted the walls a robin's-egg blue that was, she explains, "historical without being staid" and would complement the English Regency and French Louis XV pieces with which she had furnished the room. "I also put down a large rug in a rather bold leopard print," she adds. "Even with its bright walls and racy carpet, the living room still felt inviting, with plenty of comfortable seating, tables for drinks, sconces, and table lamps—all of which combined to create a pretty, even glow."

LEFT The next change included updating the chairs with fabrics that felt more contemporary. Sherrill replaced the silk damasks and dark chocolate velvet fabrics with stripes and solids in cotton and wool.

RIGHT By the early 1990s, the living room was layered with antiques of different styles, and the walls were covered in a pearlized pineapple-print paper from Rose Cumming. The nineteenth-century Chinese coromandel screen contrasted with the sofa that was upholstered in a pale Scalamandré fabric. The eighteenth-century Venetian mirror added an extra touch of glamour.

BELOW RIGHT A few years later, when Sherrill designed her first collection of furniture for Stark, she was enthusiastic about using the coffee table and sofa. "But," she explains, "to make it all work, I replaced the green-and-gold carpet with casual sisal, and removed the pineapple-print wallpaper." Inspired by the 1960s, Sherrill painted the walls a sunny, retro peach color and switched the heavy lacquered chinoiserie screen with a delicate, three-tiered Oriental cabinet. The octagonal shagreen mirror is by the designer Karl Springer.

OVERLEAF Today, the living room is elegantly restrained, thanks to the near—but not completely—perfect symmetry of the seating area. "Symmetry creates balance, and balance is essential to harmonious design," Sherrill says. The seating plan included placing an ottoman front and center, with flanking pairs of side tables, then pillows, then lamps, and finally a large mirror to reflect the room, both literally and metaphorically. The single pillow brings the accessory count up to nine. "One always wants an odd number, not an even number, of accessories," the designer says, "so that the room has an asymmetrical flourish." Painted a peachy hue, the room's palette shifted with the new orangey-brown and ivory accent colors. The geometric pillows are quieter and the sculptural floor lamps, with their braided metal bases, offer a subtle but graphic counterpoint to the ottoman.

THE NELSON A. ROCKEFELLER
MASTERPIECES OF MODERN ART

ELIZABETHAN WORLD

Vida cotidiana en las
HACIENDAS de MÉXICO

SHOWHOUSES signature designer styles

The **British Isles**

LA CIUDAD DE QUERETARO

NEW YORK APARTMENTS PrivateViews

LEFT A rattan Chinese cabinet adds an element of whimsy to the room while contrasting with the geometric-patterned pillows, one of which is made from a mitered Clarence House fabric. "I found the cabinet in a little antiques shop on Long Island and immediately fell in love with the delicate scrollwork on top," Sherrill says. The designer considers its shape a "soft counterpoint to the living room's austere, graphic edges." After bringing it home, she had the console painted a bright paprika. Made in three sections that open, the cabinet is used as a bar. "A bar is a festive yet functional addition to any living room," she says, "and this cabinet has inspired me to pull a few of my favorite antique objects, including a set of English ivory newspaper cutters and some painted chinoiserie boxes, out of storage."

OPPOSITE In its more austere transformation, the living room is clutterless—only a few well-chosen objects are on display. Sherrill's Carlton ottoman is upholstered in Interlochen in brown and cream, part of her textile collection for Old World Weavers.

OPPOSITE Hung with framed prints that came from a book on Colonial India, a pair of hurricane sconces, and the shimmery pineapple-patterned wallpaper, this now long-gone variation of a corner of the living room, Sherrill says, is "Old England with a twist." The elegant French Baguès low tables, the Knole sofa with a stylized Greek-key trim, and the eighteenth-century Italian armchair were a charmingly eclectic grouping.

ABOVE When redecorated, the living room vignette featured a different yet equally entertaining mix of furnishings: a plaster relief of an ancient battle scene, a pair of Italian tables made of zebrawood and bronze, and a pair of minimally elegant floor lamps by Cedric Hartman, the mid-century designer renowned for his modernist lighting. "Antiques and antiquities still have a place in the tailored home, " Sherrill says.

"All that is required is a little vision and a sense of humor, as well as a bit of fearlessness." The designer found the plaster relief at an antiques fair in the Hamptons and drove it home sticking out the back of her convertible. Now paired with more contemporary furnishings, the relief takes on a heroic dimension that she finds "humorous and strong."

Complete with a breakfast nook and a larger section that can accommodate a crowd, the layout of the dining room hasn't changed since the house was built in 1919, and for my purposes it happens to be ideal. One of my first tasks upon moving in was to transform the sparsely furnished nook into an area that could stand on its own. In the hope of drawing people into the dining room—my family found that it was too often neglected—I decided to make the space more inviting by installing an upholstered banquette under a curved window that overlooks the garden. Over the years, the banquette has seen new upholstery come and go, but has remained in many ways the heart of the dining room. My dining room has always featured a long, extendable mahogany table and a set of Chippendale chairs, which were the first things I purchased for the house more than twenty years ago. When I saw them, I bought them on the spot, since it's almost impossible to find a complete set of twelve antique chairs at one time. In terms of both sentiment and practicality, these chairs are irreplaceable. In keeping with my rule "when one room is crazy, the next one should be quiet," the tone of my dining room is always the opposite of the living room's. As neighbors, the two rooms are often used in tandem, and I like them to complement but not compete with each other. They may share motifs and colors, but they always differ in terms of personality. When the living room is dramatic, the dining room is demure—and vice versa, of course.

OPPOSITE A vintage photograph shows the dining room as it looked in 1919, when the house was built. In those days, the sparsely furnished breakfast nook was used for light breakfasts and tea. The main meals were served at the formal dining table.

ABOVE These days, many of the Canet family meals and small dinner parties take place around the upholstered banquette. The pleasant lighting is key: A chandelier anchors the nook, while table lamps placed on the wide windowsills create a warm, intimate atmosphere.

LEFT When the living room was undergoing its dramatic period of leopard-print carpet and robin's-egg blue walls, its more staid neighbor, the dining room, was furnished with Georgian and Victorian antiques and old-fashioned floral fabrics. Only the silk carpet, with its leopard trim, referenced the living room's more boisterous style.

BELOW LEFT AND OPPOSITE ABOVE This version of the more romantic mocha-colored dining room accompanied the living room when it was decorated in a more neutral palette of browns, golds, and creams.

OPPOSITE BELOW In its most recent incarnation, the dining room walls have been painted in a trompe l'oeil design of raised fretwork in dark raisin and white. Over the banquette, a crystal Art Deco–style chandelier replaces the traditional antique pendant.

When I want to transform a room completely, without doing a major renovation, I often turn to trompe l'oeil, a decorative painting technique. For centuries, talented artists have used blank walls as canvases, covering them with painted rolling landscapes, graphic patterns, and architectural finishes that imitate wood, marble, or limestone in a realistic fashion. Currently, my dining room walls are painted in a trompe l'oeil rendition of fretwork, punctuated by real beveled mirrors. The trellis motif was inspired by a dining room featured in a monograph of works by the prestigious Parisian decorating firm Maison Jansen. The punchy graphics are a reference to the glitz of Hollywood Regency—a style that flourished in the 1930s, or the movie-studio system's Golden Age—and give this room a vigorous, textural appeal. Today the dining room is totally changed, with the exception of the Chippendale chairs, which I've hung onto through thick and thin. I love them for their intricate, scrolled backs, which mirror the Asian motifs in my home. I like how one small detail of a design can inspire another, until a motif has worked its way through the entire house and united every room. The fact that I'm still inspired by these chairs is a testament to their timeless appeal.

OVERLEAF A beveled mirror is at the center of the trompe l'oeil fretwork panels in the dining room. Like a clear, reflective pool of water amid a dizzying display of graphics, the mirror invites the eye to relax.

There are few things I love more than a red library. No matter what sort of furnishings it's filled with, a red environment will always feel warm and enveloping, which is exactly how such a room should be. Our library is my husband's favorite room in the house, and we have a deal: It's the one room I'm not allowed to experiment with too much. Believe it or not, this is actually fine with me. No matter how modern our library gets, it will always be rooted to some extent in tradition. It's filled with deep seating, earthy materials like leather and wool, good reading lamps, and book-filled shelves. Shortly after we moved in, I fell in love with the color of a gift box from Asprey, the famous British jeweler and purveyor of designer accessories, and decided to paint the library's moldings a burgundy to match. The only hue I found that came close was a car paint, which had to be applied in fifteen coats. (The painter cried, and so did I.) But all the trouble was worth it. Twenty years later, we still love it, and I have been inspired to experiment with countless variations of unusual accent colors. In its most traditional version, the library brimmed with antiques. To soften the effect, I blended an Old World palette of burgundy, chocolate, and gold by layering pattern on pattern. The zebra-hide–framed mirror practically jumps off the wall. I love that the Asprey-box-inspired moldings have adapted to the library's changing styles: Back in the 1980s, when painted a ripe merlot, the moldings felt very traditional. Now their glossy, lacquered glaze looks glamorous and contemporary.

ABOVE LEFT AND LEFT At its most traditional, the library featured a paisley-patterned paper on the walls and a Chesterfield sofa covered in shiny burgundy leather. A vintage Vuitton trunk is used as a coffee table and functions as a casual counterpoint to the more formal pieces dominating the room. Antlers hung on the walls imparted a masculine vibe.

RIGHT By the 1990s, an English Bridgewater sofa covered in red mohair velvet from Old World Weavers had replaced the Chesterfield. And instead of the paisley paper, the walls were now upholstered in a bold, graphic stripe from F. Schumacher, which imparted a quietness and warmth. Some leopard pillows and urn lamps topped with custom shades in peacock blue add both personality and color to the room. A pair of club chairs has been upholstered in a camel-colored wool from Pollack.

BELOW RIGHT Most recently, the zebra-covered frame of the mirror and a pair of modern tables give the room a more contemporary look. According to Sherrill, "The lighting in a library should always be low and cozy, so skip pendants and chandeliers in favor of plenty of table and floor lamps— preferably with silk shades, and always on dimmers."

Like most people, I want my bedroom to be as peaceful as possible, so I chose a soft, charming palette in ivory and powder blue and immediately installed wall-to-wall carpeting to block out noise and keep the room warm. Over the years, the colors of my bedroom have not changed very much. I picked a headboard that could be accessorized with different bed linens and chose mirrored and silver gilt furniture with a soft, romantic look that would be perfect in any master bedroom.

LEFT Years ago, the bed in the Canets' master bedroom was crowned with a simple silk curtain, rather than the more typical old-fashioned canopy. The custom-made headboard was upholstered in a durable chocolate brown Scalamandré horsehair fabric, and trimmed with blue satin and nailheads. The mirrored night tables are from Julia Gray; the swing-arm lamps from the Christopher Norman Collection. The painted antique bench at the foot of the bed is handy for stacking pillows and books.

LEFT AND OPPOSITE For a sleeker look, to which the existing headboard was easily adapted, a Chinese Art Deco panel was hung behind the bed. The room's temperament changed when the graphic set of plaid bed linens in camel, chocolate, and ivory was substituted for the needlepoint pillow and powder blue duvet. The table lamp is from Ralph Lauren.

If my bedroom is romantic and serene, then the guest bedroom is often a wild card. It should be inviting but surprising, as opposed to a room you want to live in every day. But some of the rules that apply to the master bedroom work here, too. Wall-to-wall carpeting is a great idea, and good lighting is essential. But in terms of palette, headboard, and furniture, I like to let loose and experiment. Although you may not choose to have a television in the master bedroom, you should consider having one in the guest room.

LEFT Documented in 1919, the guest bedroom was rather sedate and traditional, its style in keeping with the rest of the house, which was furnished with English and American antiques. Rugs surrounded the four-poster bed, and other pieces included a Windsor rocker and an armchair pulled up to a secretary.

BELOW LEFT A contemporary four-poster from Baker pays tribute to the original one that was the focus of the guest room nearly a century ago. Sherrill's choice of a black border on the draperies and pelmet, the bold Chinese calligraphy print from Andrew Martin on the settee, and a faux-leopard throw, contribute to the room's lively, dramatic look.

OPPOSITE The painted table, straw boxes, antique Oxblood table lamp, and bold calligraphic fabric from Andrew Martin, as well as walls glazed deep red, turn the guest room into a jewel box.

In my home, the family room is where everyone congregates, so I choose materials like chenille, cotton, and outdoor fabrics that can handle heavy traffic. Fortunately, you don't have to sacrifice beauty for durability. One of the biggest trends in decorating today is an idea I call the luxury of low maintenance. Nearly all my clients want gorgeous fabrics that can withstand the elements, and by "elements," I'm sure they mean children and pets.

OPPOSITE Sherrill added the mantelpiece where the stove had been located and had the chaise upholstered in ivory chenille and edged with leather piping. The organic Amazon table, with its gilded wood base and glass top, is by the designer and available from Stark. The zebra-print carpet is both decorative and practical. "Dark patterned carpets are the best defense against dirty paws and spilled drinks," she says.

RIGHT Once the house's original kitchen, the den, now furnished with modular sofas, is perfect for movie nights. The abstract geometric Caning pattern in walnut is from Sherrill's collection of Sunbrella fabrics for Old World Weavers. The photograph is by Kleinfelder; the custom-made table is covered in chocolate-and-ivory hide.

Outdoor rooms—especially those overlooking the Long Island Sound—have a rich history on the Gold Coast. These rooms were furnished like interiors and included comfortable seating and soft lighting, so that guests could congregate and mingle on summer nights, long before the days of air-conditioning. Inspired by this loggia, I set to work designing a terraced room of my own.

ABOVE Beneath the grand arches of Caumsett, a 1920s mansion in Lloyd Neck, New York, that once belonged to Marshall Field III, guests enjoyed prime views of the water from the rear loggia. A deep awning swept the perimeter to protect guests from the sun while allowing breezes to cool the terrace.

ABOVE The informal terrace outside the living room
at Sherrill's house is furnished with overscale rattan
armchairs and has pillows and upholstery made from
black-and-white–striped outdoor fabric. The hanging
glass lantern allows the space to be used in the
evening; black-edged curtains protect the space in
inclement weather.

2 ESSENTIALS FOR CREATING AN OLD WORLD ATMOSPHERE

STYLE SHEET 2: CHIPPENDALE, CHINOISERIE, SWAGS, AND FRINGE

Traditional style is the peak of Old World decorating. I want to be very clear: an Old World look need not be boring, but it does involve taking history into consideration. For inspiration, I scour the past, looking at classical architecture and historical rooms for direction on everything from moldings and textiles to lighting and accessories.

A mid-eighteenth century painted breakfront bookcase, from Kentshire Galleries in New York, a section of which is shown above, was inspired by the designs of the premier English cabinetmaker Thomas Chippendale, with their interplay of rococo, chinoiserie, and gothic motifs. Here the cabinetmaker took extra liberties, creating a more exuberant and playful piece of furniture.

The Old World palette is rich and deep—a well-blended mix of historical colors like peacock blue, burgundy, pine green, or navy—with generous accents of gold, right.

I advise my clients to find periods and objects that inspire them—French or English antiques, Elizabethan brocades, Gothic architectural features, the opulence of Louis XV or rococo—and let them be their guide.

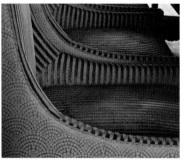

Luxurious textiles such as silks and velvets work best in this style. Don't hold back on details: Swags, trims, and embroidery are wonderfully opulent touches for creating a grand Old World style.

I also like to look at images from English country houses, left, and their bygone pastimes such as foxhunting, below. A dog painting, below, can also provide atmosphere. My frame of reference is book-ended by the sixteenth and the nineteenth centuries, with everything in between up for grabs.

Like a big, boisterous bow, window treatments, below, complete a room. Use tiebacks and bullion fringe for drama.

My most important advice is this: When choosing furniture, don't stick to one period. A room that's all English Victorian, or all French Provincial, can feel strange today. Instead mix periods, provenance, and styles. For dimension, add rich patterns in fabrics, below, or rugs, below right.

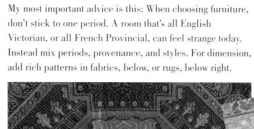

Correct lighting can make any room look good. To get soft, even light, mix sconces, table lamps, floor lamps, and chandeliers that incorporate traditional materials such as bronze, brass, porcelain, iron, or glass.

The trick to pairings is about picking pieces that complement one another in terms of scale, color, and detail as in this New York showhouse room for cancer research, below.

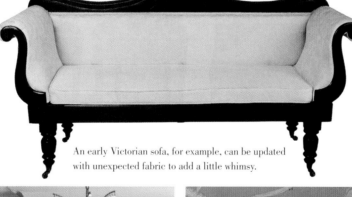

An early Victorian sofa, for example, can be updated with unexpected fabric to add a little whimsy.

Top lamps with shades that are fringed, pleated, or feathered—the more detailing, the better.

Besides layering period styles, try layering formal elements with casual ones. You might combine ornate, gilded frames and a crystal chandelier with needlepoint pillows, and sisal. Position a few exotic curiosities among your crystal and porcelain objects. When artfully arranged, this clutter shows personality and makes your home feel lived-in. Finally, make chinoiserie accessories, left, in all shapes and sizes, your new best friend. The delicate motifs on cabinets, textiles, and accessories bring balance to a room filled with European antiques.

Inspired by a vintage photograph of an entry hall from an early-twentieth-century mansion in Oyster Bay, New York, I set about furnishing a similar space for one of my clients who had commissioned the New York architect Oliver Cope to build a very grand neo-Gothic-style house featuring an imposing exterior ornamented with spires and turrets. With its high ceilings and sweeping staircase, the architecture of the entry hall was well on its way to making an impression to match the exterior. All I needed to do was apply the finishing touches.

LEFT The two-story entry hall—with its dramatic staircase, its walls carved of English Yorkshire stone, and a late-fifteenth-century English tapestry that once belonged to J. P. Morgan—was one of the most dramatic areas in La Selva ("the forest" in Italian), a Mediterranean-style villa designed around 1915 by the architectural firm of Hunt and Hunt in Oyster Bay, New York, for Henry Sanderson, a prominent New York financier.

OPPOSITE The high ceilings give a sense of scale while the stairway makes a bold, opulent gesture in this contemporary incarnation of Gothic style. Limestone floors, walls treated in Venetian plaster, a custom-made bronze-and-iron handrail, a sixteenth-century wool and silk tapestry from the Persian Gallery, New York, and an overscale glass-and-bronze lantern from Marvin Alexander in New York create a sense of Old World grandeur in a recently built home on Long Island.

LEFT Gothic archways add architectural authenticity and symmetry to the entry hall, which is bathed in natural light, thanks to an opaque glass skylight overhead. Anchoring the generously proportioned space is a classic center hall table, an English Georgian beauty from Florian Papp in New York. The large bouquet of white hydrangea in a chinoiserie vase creates a lovely focal point.

OPPOSITE The scrolled baroque pattern of the stair runner is in mocha, burgundy, ivory, and blue. It was made by Hokanson, a company that specializes in custom-designed, handmade carpets.

I keep landings well furnished, since people are always passing through. Even if the furniture is rarely used, a couple of chairs, a console, lamps, and fresh flowers will keep the space from feeling awkward or empty.

LEFT AND OPPOSITE The pattern of the stair runner extends to the upper landing for a sense of continuity. Gothic-style side chairs covered in a burgundy-and-ivory cut velvet from Nobilis and an eighteenth-century–style penwork-decorated console, a centuries-old painting technique that imitates ivory inlay, were added to the long hall. Two antique cast-iron, urn-shaped lamps stand near an overscale print that depicts a flamboyant grille, and work beautifully to tie together the various decorative elements.

Original details like arched windows, plaster moldings, and a marble fireplace infuse any living room with authentic elegance. For a well-bred atmosphere that won't feel stuffy, I need to assemble a seamless mix of formal and casual designs. Allowing the architecture to guide my choices, I pick a careful assortment of antiques, balancing statement pieces with subtle classics for an effect that is neither garish nor dull. Often I add traditional ingredients with personalities that range from quiet to loud, starting with sisal carpeting and simple, timeless upholstery.

RIGHT The living room in this New York City duplex in a 1907 building on Gramercy Park features a central seating area focused around the fireplace and complemented by classic upholstery. Accompanying the plush, traditional chairs is an English Regency carved-gilt armchair and numerous side tables, as well as a round Regency table. The silk pillows and the sisal rug from Stark are casual and unexpected compared with the room's more formal look. For a contrasting effect, Sherrill hung an Old Master painting of Leda and the Swan that her clients found in Europe, and an eighteenth-century French gilt mirror. She also mixed antique lighting with interesting accessories such as gilt sconces, onyx lamps, bronze busts, footed bowls, and vintage prints. To frame the arched windows, she designed elegant drapes of ivory silk with black silk banding.

I designed this living room's color palette—a quite extraordinary salmon, chocolate, and powder blue—to be a fresh and airy backdrop for its antique furnishings. Light and ethereal, the colors turn the room, with its eighteenth-century pieces and over-the-top detailing that impart a serious mood, into a more upbeat and memorable space.

RIGHT The living room is filled with meticulously executed details: raised moldings, custom-made fringed-silk lamp shades, and a hand-embroidered silk velvet ottoman by Penn & Fletcher in New York. A change of scale breathes dimension into the room, from the tiniest stitch to the delicate pale-blue strié finish on the walls.

LEFT AND OPPOSITE "I wanted the Swedish Gustavian settee to explode out of the room's dreamy palette," Sherrill says of the magnificent brown-and-white–striped silk from Clarence House on the long, low sofa. "I loved how the fabric contrasted with everything in the room but at the same time pulled it all together. It was one of those moments in decorating when you have to trust your eye: You see something beautiful and it just makes sense, even if it bends or breaks the rules," the designer explains. In a counterpoint to the sofa's graphic silk stripes, Sherrill added pillows made from rare antique textiles.

This formal living room in a traditional house on Long Island was inspired in part by an old Parisian apartment I once visited. Brimming with pattern, detail, and a lifetime of objects and antiques found at flea markets, small shops, and antiques fairs, the apartment made decorating look easy. I thought of Sister Parish, the great interior decorator who put together objects because she liked them, not because they necessarily matched. Inspired by her free-spirited sense of style, I assembled this room piece by piece, pairing my clients' heirloom objects with newly discovered antiques and unusual vintage textiles.

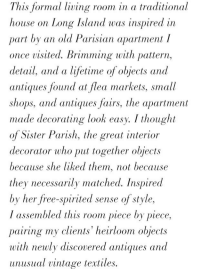

OPPOSITE A pair of antique Chinese vases from Kentshire Galleries in New York decorate the eighteenth-century carved stone mantel.

ABOVE LEFT Fashion textiles like this metallic floral brocade that Sherrill chose for the drapes add a stylish edge. A chunky tassel tieback and an antique eighteenth-century hall chair complete a vignette that adds to the room's glamorous look.

ABOVE The intricately embroidered upholstery of the carved French stool coordinates well with the muted antique rug from Darius.

When I'm asked to create a library, many of my clients are inspired by libraries in English country houses, where men traditionally gathered after dinner to smoke cigars and drink brandy. My interpretation of Old World libraries evokes the color palette, furnishings, and materials of the atmospheric rooms of the past without looking like a pastiche of the style.

After gathering ideas from bygone sporting traditions such as foxhunting and sailing, I often choose hearty, masculine colors like red, gold, and chocolate brown; natural materials such as walnut, leather, brass, and horn; and warm, old-fashioned textiles including velvet and wool. Plenty of deep seating and excellent reading lamps are important. And to keep things from feeling too staid, I like to add unusual textures. Especially with a crackling fire in the winter, a traditional library offers a wonderful respite from the outside world.

ABOVE New York architect Oliver Cope designed this ultimate gentleman's library in a Long Island home. Sherrill furnished the room with polished French walnut cabinetry and antique leather-bound books. Shelves encircle the room, adding coziness and a feeling of seclusion.

ABOVE The custom tufted-leather fender provides a
warm seat by the fire; the eighteenth-century–style
English sofa is upholstered in cut velvet. A deep
club chair, complete with ottoman, is a great place
to curl up in. For a crisp, graphic foundation, a silk
trellis-patterned carpet by Hokanson was chosen
over the more usual antique Oriental.

ABOVE A club chair upholstered in a deep red velvet from Scalamandré is accessorized with an opulent antique textile pillow. The antique bronze standing lamp is conveniently placed for reading. Scalamandré velvet draperies trimmed in a metallic Fortuny fabric hang from high rods and filter the light from the French windows overlooking the garden.

ABOVE Shelves filled with books and interesting accessories such as framed wax seals and small bronze urns create a rich backdrop for the room.

ABOVE Antique tasseled tapestry pillows are a good match for the gold-and-red hues in Scalamandré's strié velvet that covers the sofa in another of Sherrill's inviting libraries.

ABOVE Pillows made from haberdashery-inspired prints from Ralph Lauren are a casual counterpoint to the cut velvet upholstery.

For a more contemporary house on the Gold Coast, I designed a red library to be punchy and youthful, with brighter colors and strong graphic elements that contrast with the walnut bookshelves, which are traditional and grounding. This room was for a young couple that wanted to bring in some of their mementos, including interesting objects made from horn and hide, as well as the library's centerpiece, a contemporary oil painting of a ship—a testament to its adventurous owners. Unlike my traditional libraries, this room is a bit more edgy, *incorporating pieces of antique coral, chinoiserie, and bright-red hues. The wool-and-suede carpet in a trellis pattern from Beauvais grounds the extraordinary details of the room.*

LEFT AND ABOVE Adorned with decorative bronze-and-zinc panels, the library's mantel features a display of objects from the natural world, including tusks on Lucite stands and a paprika-dyed cowhide mirror frame studded with rows of nailheads. The seating by the fireplace is smart-looking, with Art Deco club chairs and an ebony-and-quill table.

Given the opportunity to create a spacious game room, I decided to exaggerate and play with another variation of Old World style. My client liked the idea of re-creating a medieval hunting hall that felt current and upbeat. Instead of adding a lot of antique statement pieces, I decided to paint the room's remarkable architectural woodwork—including the built-in corner cabinets and the Gothic mantel, all designed by architect Oliver Cope—to make them the primary attraction. In a bright peacock blue, the potentially grandiose architecture sheds its seriousness to inject the room with a memorable element of surprise.

ABOVE To keep the large room from feeling disjointed, the palette was restricted to three colors: peacock blue, paprika, and gold. The woodwork, treated in this vibrant, playful way, allows the oversize mantel to seem less imposing. The large custom-made ottoman, covered in an animal print from Jane Shelton, doubles as a coffee table.

ABOVE The furniture pieces were chosen for their personality. For example, the scrolled-back bar stool from Minton-Spidell, placed between the window and the billiard table, looks like it belongs in an Austrian hunting lodge.

ABOVE Instead of upholstering the fire fender in leather, Sherrill used the same fabric pattern she chose for the embroidered curtains by Penn & Fletcher, but in a different scale and color. By repeating the motif in a slightly different version, her objective was to create continuity in the space without making it feel overly coordinated.

The seating arrangements around the areas of activity, like the fireplace, the game tables, the television, and especially the windows—everyone likes to look at the pretty view—were designed to be comfortable and inviting. One way I achieved this atmosphere was by mixing the patterns and materials to create an uncontrived decor. I paired cut velvets with haberdashery plaids, and an Oriental rug with velvets and leather. The blond finish of the yew wood paneling is masculine, though without the heaviness of walnut or mahogany.

LEFT The inglenook, a traditional seating configuration built around a fireplace for cocktails and conversation, features yew wood paneling, benches, and an ottoman covered in a burgundy-and-white cut velvet from Sanderson.

OPPOSITE Architectural details like vaulted archways and paneled bay windows lend gravitas to any game room. In this large space, a pair of low wing chairs upholstered in Jeu de Cartes, a cotton needlepoint from Clarence House, and a leather-wrapped table, are perfect for quiet conversations. Armchairs covered in a Robert Allen Ultrasuede are pulled up to two long tables that function for both gin games and casual dining. A Watts of Westminster graphic black-and-white medallion-design fabric, which mimics a dapper dress shirt or blazer, gives the curtains a playful, boyish feel.

OVERLEAF The graphic playing card pattern of the Jeu de Cartes fabric from Clarence House covers the large ottoman and offers a lively counterpoint to the classic Oriental carpet from Stark.

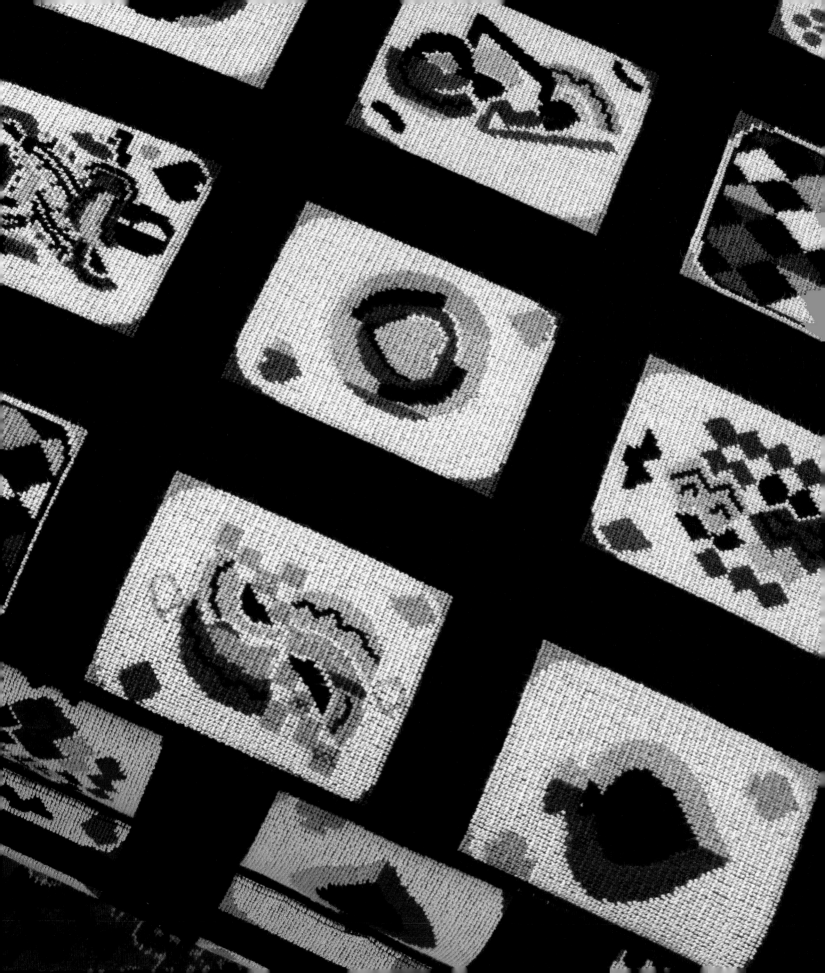

Lighting plays a key part in a home, especially in a traditional, formal dining room. Even if the table seats a large group, the room should feel intimate. Different levels of light—overhead chandeliers, lamps whose light is filtered through silk shades, and sconces—all contribute to an overall romantic glow. I also like to treat the ceiling of a dining room with a metallic or softly colored paper.

LEFT In this formal dining room, Sherrill had the walls upholstered in a gaufraged mohair velvet from Bergamo. "You can't imagine how a fabric wall treatment affects the acoustics of a room—it's like being inside a cocoon!" she explains. The overscale pattern of gold dahlias on a celadon silk background from Jim Thompson, the famous Thai company, covers the seventeenth-century–style Italian chair. As the dahlias are similar in scale to the vine motif of the wall fabric, the two are compatible. "It's as if they both came from the same garden," Sherrill says.

OPPOSITE For an effect that's impromptu and effortless, a mix of dining chairs surrounds the Regency-style table. The painted Italian commode plays off the room's floral patterns and is convenient for serving. A crystal chandelier from Marvin Alexander, one of Sherrill's favorite sources in New York, twinkles overhead. The china, a combination of two patterns, Jardins de Florence and Toscane, is from Philippe Deshoulières.

Located in a large country home designed by Oliver Cope and with windows that look out to the Long Island Sound, my clients planned to use this dining room for special events like holidays and dinner parties. They wanted the room to feel exotic, to be a space that would sweep guests away to another time and place, like Venice or Paris in the eighteenth century. With their vision in mind, I chose a hand-painted wallpaper and accented its historical teal coloring with ivory and apricot tones. I also brought in furnishings to suit a traditional dining room, including elaborate curtains with sumptuous swags and tassels, a huge, festive crystal chandelier, and an extending mahogany table.

OPPOSITE AND OVERLEAF Hand-painted with a graceful Chinese garden motif, the wallpaper from De Gournay in London is the star of the room. In the evening, the space—bathed in light from the crystal chandelier, the French 1940s Baguès sconces, and the tall candles—allows "for everyone to look their best," Sherrill says. The eighteenth-century French gilt mirror enhances the romantic ambience.

RIGHT The built-in niche to the right of the fireplace displays an heirloom collection of Imari porcelain. The ornately carved French armchair in apricot leather and the English Victorian fire screen are lovely touches.

OPPOSITE Swags and bullion fringe add to the lushness of the draperies.

RIGHT The chinoiserie cabinet and porcelain vases, decorative counterpoints to the room's weightier mahogany dining table and leather-wrapped chairs, also complement the delicacy of the flowered wallpaper.

I have an ongoing love affair with chinoiserie cabinets, which possess a delicacy lacking in many European antiques. If you ever stop to wonder what might be missing in a room filled with antiques from England and France, it's most likely one of these pieces. But chinoiserie cabinets are not all actually from China. The term chinoiserie refers to a style of decoration that developed in seventeenth-century Europe, when a cultural fascination with the Far East began. Dazzled by the prowess of Chinese and Japanese decorative arts, particularly lacquerware and ceramics, European artisans rushed to imitate them, conjuring fanciful scenes and images of an imaginary Far East, which they applied to vases, dishes, tea sets, and, of course, cabinets. I like to include at least one chinoiserie cabinet in every traditional home I design, though some clients need a bit more convincing than others. Adorned or painted with whimsical gold imagery and fabulous hardware, these cabinets—usually brick red or black—are available in many shapes and sizes. A tall one adds height to a space, while a heftier version can anchor a room. These pieces not only make dramatic statements, but they are functional, too, multitasking as bars, desks, and places to store special small and treasured pieces of silver, ivory, or porcelain. When it comes to buying a chinoiserie piece, there are plenty of fabulous reproductions to be found. But nothing can compare to an authentic antique.

OPPOSITE Placed under the stairwell of an entrance hall, this eighteenth-century brown-lacquered chest stands on an elegant rattan stand.

ABOVE RIGHT A reproduction can be wonderful, too. This Georgian-style secretary is from the Lewis Mittman company.

RIGHT After years of looking for the perfect piece for a special living room, Sherrill found this eighteenth-century Italian secretary in San Francisco. "By the middle of the eighteenth century," she explains, "chinoiserie would inform rococo, an ornate decorative style that was just beginning to flourish. With its fanciful shape and painted imagery that are distinctly European, this cabinet is an excellent example of how the two styles merged."

Considering how advanced technology is today, an Old World kitchen may seem like a contradiction in terms. But if you choose the right palette, detailing, and hardware, then the most innovative kitchen in the world can exude a timeless, traditional demeanor. Working with architect Oliver Cope, I paired elements such as marble and black granite with champagne-colored subway tiles and bronze hardware. To further distinguish the kitchen, the island was made into the space's focal point, grounding the room without weighing it down.

RIGHT The large kitchen, in a newly built house on Long Island, effortlessly melds modern equipment with an Old World aesthetic and neo-Gothic architectural detailing. A pair of tole chandeliers from Vaughan hangs over the large center island. The upper cabinets are faced in leaded, seeded glass to lighten the effect of the custom woodwork. The creamy, textured subway tiles are from Ann Sachs; the knobs, from Katonah Architectural Hardware. The stove was made to order from La Cornue, the hundred-year-old French company.

3 ELEMENTS THAT CONTRIBUTE TO A DECOR FULL OF CHARM

STYLE SHEET 3: CREATING A HOME FULL OF CHARM

A home that enchants is rooted in tradition but dips into the twentieth and twenty-first centuries for added inspiration and oomph. In terms of style, the frame of reference starts with the nineteenth century and ends at the Art Deco era. Depending on how you live, the look can be customized to suit a country house or an urban high-rise.

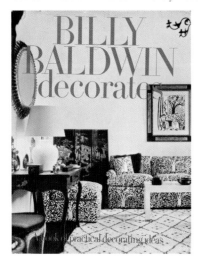

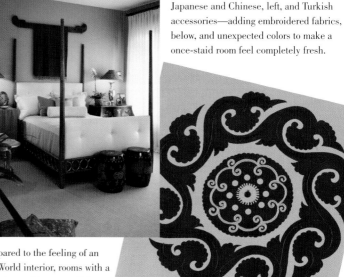

I also like to combine traditional furnishings with American arts and crafts pieces, Japanese and Chinese, left, and Turkish accessories—adding embroidered fabrics, below, and unexpected colors to make a once-staid room feel completely fresh.

Billy Baldwin's bag of design tricks, above, which I routinely dip into for guidance, brims with bold combinations of color, styles and materials, all of which helped lay the groundwork for modern decorating. The most important requirement for this style is a little imagination. You have to trust your instincts and operate on a dare.

Groundbreaking firms from the early- to mid-twentieth-century, like the French Maison Jansen (their Paris bedroom for cosmetics queen Helena Rubinstein is above) often inspire me.

Compared to the feeling of an Old World interior, rooms with a charming ambience are lighter, with ethereal pastel palettes of violet, silver, peach, or celadon, below.

Seek out wall treatments like hand-painted murals, above, or faux finishes that replicate animal hides or opalescent oyster shells. And try to include one wild splash of unexpected color, such as in the photograph below.

Simple draperies of pale, subtly patterned silk from Bergamo, a mid-century Murano glass half-cylinder sconce, and the subdued profile of the dining chair complement the wallpaper, above right.

Depending on the mix created, the style can feel urbane—think about Art Deco with a touch of Asia and a zebra print, right—or more sophisticated and country-like, such as antique French chairs, upholstered in white cotton, as shown in a Parisian room by Frédéric Mechiche, left.

The furniture in a charm-filled house is a thoughtful mix of styles from all over the world, with at least one totally wonderful piece that pushes the room from conventional to exceptional. My Kensington chair is below.

Carpets of all styles, from an antique silk to a casual sisal, below, work well. What matters is how the furnishings are layered on top of the rugs.

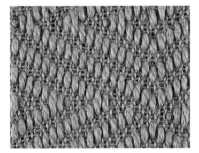

A similar rule applies to textiles: Anything goes, as long as the elements are layered properly. I love silks and velvets, especially when they are paired with something contemporary, like this fabric from F. Schumacher on the armchair, above.

Painted furniture, right, brings a sense of understated elegance to a home: its delicate garden motifs pair beautifully with a light palette, a sisal carpet, and silk and embroidered textiles.

An extravagant bouquet of tall delphiniums blooming in a Chinese Export porcelain vase can add sparkle to any room. I love a boisterous arrangement of flowers. It's also a great way to add personality to a space.

LEFT Wanting to lift a foyer out of its traditional framework of parquet floors and antique sconces, Sherrill upholstered a curved Regency settee in brilliant aquamarine silk-velvet from Scalamandré. Repeated in the custom-made medallion carpet and stair runner, the shade carries through the entry hall and up the stairs to the landing. "You can transform a space with one vibrant color," Sherrill says.

OPPOSITE Designed by Sherrill and custom-made by Hokanson, the runner offers a warm, tonal palette of mocha and chocolate with aquamarine accents. The vibrant stroke of blue adds depth to the limestone floors and brightens the iron-and-bronze banister.

Even when it's of the highest quality, painted furniture allows the creation of an informal design that is pretty, charming, and feminine. I use such furnishings, traditionally found in the old country manors of Europe, to lighten up an otherwise serious room or as a contrast to dark mahogany pieces. I also like to juxtapose painted furniture with textiles that exude a feeling of country elegance—silk, linen, wool, and in some cases leather—in solid colors or light, delicate designs. Painted furniture is also stunning when paired with an array of mercury glass, one of my favorite accessories for drumming up glamour.

OPPOSITE Graced with intricate gilt work, this armchair dates from the eighteenth century. The chair's upholstery—a wide ruby red and turquoise stripe—reflects the rosy pinks of the delicate flowers on the painted console.

RIGHT Although less formal in feeling, this eighteenth-century painted Italian console is a fortuitous match to a pair of museum-quality nineteenth-century porcelain vases. Sherrill found the set of antique botanical prints during a shopping trip in London.

RIGHT Color dictated the ambience of this New York City living room, which Sherrill designed for a young couple. Bathed in silver, violet, and white, the palette, Sherrill says, is unexpected, serene, and sophisticated—an example of how modern colors can completely update a traditional room. The different textures exert a similar effect, putting a youthful spin on antiques for a mix that is fresh and free-spirited. An antique bergère is covered in a white Edelman leather; the coffee table, from Sri Lanka, is inlaid with bone; zebra hide is used on the ottoman; and on the walls, a faux finish of mother-of-pearl casts a burnished glow. Elegant silk drapes, tied back with custom-made tassels and metallic passementerie, and the silk upholstery, offer an interesting contrast to the natural texture of the sisal carpet.

OVERLEAF In a Long Island living room inspired by a traditional French salon, the sofas and armchairs in soft tonal fabrics are demure and comfortable, while the bright velvet pillows and the contemporary glass-topped cocktail table provide unexpected touches. Over the mantel hangs an early-nineteenth-century Chinese embroidered-silk textile; the nineteenth-century–style lacquered chinoiserie secretary is a reproduction from Edward Ferrell–Lewis Mittman. "In this kind of living room," Sherrill says, "I tend to keep the style more traditional, adding flourishes that range from the eighteenth century to the 1920s and 1930s. I rely on luxurious textures—silks, velvets, wools—and painted furniture to create a rather grand but understated elegance and charm."

OPPOSITE Taking her cue from the formal English gardens that surround this Long Island house, Sherrill had a lattice motif in pale blue and ivory painted on the domed ceiling of the breakfast room, which is often also used for lunch and dinner. The trompe l'oeil artwork by Mark Skinner of Skinner Interiors in Brooklyn, New York, creates the illusion of looking through a garden trellis up to the sky. The lantern is from Vaughan.

RIGHT Textiles inspired by botanicals were chosen for the dining chairs, but a measure of restraint was in order. The klismos-style chairs, from Artistic Frame, have their fronts and seats upholstered in a Lee Jofa printed cotton, and their backs covered in a wool from Holland & Sherry. From behind, the chairs look quiet and sleek beneath the opulent ceiling. When pulled out from the table, they take on a lively air, recalling a country garden in bloom.

Unlike an Old World dining room, which is by definition unequivocally formal, the dining room most suitable for a charming country home should feel more relaxed. To create a sense of effortless elegance, I choose one special element and then tone it down with other objects. In this dining room, which I designed for a young family, I picked a striking hand-painted Gracie wallpaper of a silvery-gold bamboo forest on a deep chocolate background. The paper became the room's singular statement. Depending on the star piece chosen—an antique dining table or a wonderfully patterned carpet, for example—other furnishings, such as the dining chairs and a cabinet or console, can play supporting roles. An overhead

light source—plus sconces, candles, and table lamps—are essential, since excellent, balanced lighting heightens the ambience. Finally, beautiful china and porcelain, a mirror or two to expand and reflect light, and room for art are also important considerations.

ABOVE Sherrill chose an abstract painting to contrast with the paper's elaborate, decorative style. "A classical landscape would have made the wallpaper feel more proper," Sherrill says. "This pairing feels more current, more mod."

ABOVE One of a pair in the room, the metal Brighton étagère was designed by Sherrill for Stark. Its pagoda shape refers to the Asian feel of the wallpaper and the lanterns and is further enhanced by a collection of antique Chinese Export pieces.

OPPOSITE A farmhouse-style table from Holly Hunt and contemporary dining chairs covered in powder blue Robert Allen Ultrasuede were chosen for their durability. The sisal carpet adds to the casual look and, Sherrill says, "stabilizes the wallpaper. "A pair of pagoda-style lanterns from Holly Hunt is a less conventional choice than a single chandelier."

OVERLEAF "I put all my lighting theories to work in this dining room," Sherrill explains. "To the primary light source—the Holly Hunt lanterns—I added a pair of porcelain table lamps with brown silk shades with white-piping trim and, for entertaining in the evening, rock crystal votives." With its mottled glass, the tall French, custom-made mirror above the yellow Sloane console, another of Sherrill's designs for Stark, makes the room feel brighter and more spacious.

No matter the style, bedrooms—and master bedrooms in particular—should feel serene, quiet, and comforting. It's nice to add a touch of romance to nearly every element of the decor, from the color palette to the furnishings and bed linens. In most bedrooms, it's best to start with the most basic element: wall-to-wall carpeting, preferably in a neutral color, to keep the room quiet and warm. After that's in place, I build a soft range of garden colors: pale blue, ivory, celadon, light rose, and silver. I also believe that in any bedroom, the bed should always be the main event. I like to adorn it with a graceful canopy or an upholstered headboard, which can be accessorized with a vintage screen or a striking painting. Embroidered vintage linens and quilts can make the room feel even more inviting. For nightstands, I prefer painted or parchment-wrapped furniture for their softness. Excellent lighting for reading in bed is a must. I usually choose a pair of vintage lamps. Also, try to place a desk or sitting area near a window or around the fireplace.

OPPOSITE The base of a custom-made desk in the corner of a Long Island bedroom has been wrapped in a gold-and-russet–printed cotton from Groves Bros., a fabric company based in Fort Worth, Texas. An Italian lamp, a framed mirror, and a 1940s armchair heighten the creamy pale peach, ivory, and mocha palette of the room.

ABOVE RIGHT For Sherrill, "this master bedroom combines the best of pastoral romance and city elegance." Beneath an antique Japanese screen is a linen-upholstered, nailhead-trimmed headboard. Flanking it is a pair of parchment-covered Monroe nightstands designed by Sherrill for Stark. The ceramic lamps are by Christopher Spitzmiller in New York.

RIGHT The vintage embroidered pillow is from Virginia Di Sciascio, a shop in New York.

PREVIOUS PAGES A carved limestone mantel in a spacious master bedroom features a series of unusual and romantic objects. Victorian spoon warmers in the shape of seashells hold white garden roses, and the small fire screens, also Victorian, are trimmed in silk fringe. An eighteenth-century English mirror features delicate blue glass appliqués.

ABOVE The bedroom, whose walls are glazed in celadon, is focused around a four-poster bed from Julia Gray that has been draped with a charming silk-trimmed canopy. A Biedermeier armoire from Iliad Antiques in New York is flanked by a collection of sanguine pastel drawings and a pair of Louis XVI armchairs upholstered in embroidered silk.

ABOVE The pattern of the Stark carpet, in a
geometric floral repeat, and the flowering vine-
patterned fabric on the fringed ottoman are similar in
scale and color, but have different personalities,
which, Sherrill says, "makes them a good match."

OPPOSITE By a sunny window, a reading nook is furnished with a tufted-velvet window seat and an old-fashioned chaise with a tasseled bolster and pillows. The curtains, trimmed in blue-and-white rickrack, complement the chaise's starburst-patterned fabric.

ABOVE Sherrill furnished an exuberant bedroom for a young girl with four-poster beds, floral shaped fringed ottomans, Italian chairs, and a French armoire. The carpet is from Stark and the walls have been hand-painted.

OPPOSITE "Ciel de lits are so dramatic and fun," Sherrill says, describing the canopy treatment that crowns the bed in this Gold Coast guest room. "They are perfect for a special guest bedroom." The bullion-fringed canopy comprises two different fabrics, a floral brocade lined in a small-scale woven pattern. The demilune nightstands are antiques.

ABOVE A room for a little girl is fresh and sophisticated. Sherrill bought new mirrors and had them painted a bright pink. "They bring just the right amount of playfulness to the pair of classic, painted French beds," she says. A pair of tufted, flower-shaped ottomans and a hot pink, gourd-shaped table lamp from Robert Abbey are whimsical additions.

ABOVE Upholstered in a hot pink cotton, the carved wood frame of the chaise has been matched to a wallpaper with a pattern of wildflowers.

4 INGREDIENTS THAT MAKE UP A CHIC TAILORED LOOK

STYLE SHEET 4: THE SECRETS OF TAILORED CHIC

For me, spare, comfortable, and totally glamorous, the elegant modern interior is a natural development from traditional decorating. My reference points range from the 1920s through the present, with special emphasis on American Art Deco, French Moderne, and Hollywood Regency, which I love for its high-contrast combinations of fussy with sleek, loud with quiet, and dark with light.

One of my longtime icons has been Jean-Michel Frank, who covered his walls and avant-garde furniture designs in exotic dyed leathers, above, and shagreen, below.

My style heroes include the fabulous Dorothy Draper, above, whose dramatic eye for color and contrast pioneered an imaginative baroque style in New York in the 1940s.

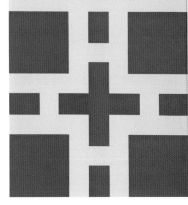

I often think of the great English designer David Hicks, who created strikingly graphic fabrics and carpets, and proved that one could successfully combine contemporary patterns with classical antiques.

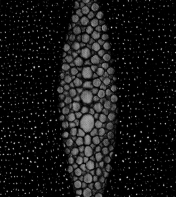

Contrast is the linchpin of the tailored look; it's also a modus operandi for breaking every rule in the decorating handbook.

A pared-down palette is monochromatic or shockingly bright. Accent a single color like champagne with metals, mirrors, and a spot of red. Or pair vivid colors—royal blue, emerald green, or chrome yellow—with white, below.

One of my favorite pairings is chocolate and white, sometimes with a hit of tangerine.

Contrast extends to prints inspired by geometry and modern art. Some of my designs for Old World Weavers are above.

My favorite materials for this style include linen, leather, wool, suede, and chenille, above. I love finishing an upholstered piece with piping or nailheads, or adding unexpected accessories such as shells and coral, right.

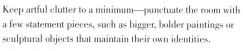

Keep artful clutter to a minimum—punctuate the room with a few statement pieces, such as bigger, bolder paintings or sculptural objects that maintain their own identities.

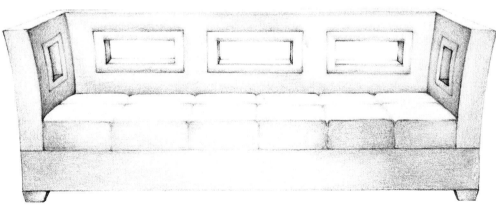

The furniture in this contemporary style is clean, spare, and unfussy. I like to compose an abstract form of pattern by juxtaposing textures like subtly patterned carpets, embossed velvets, and damasks, with unexpected touches of gilt, right.

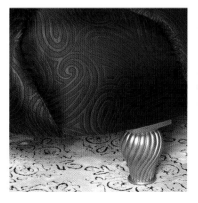

My Eaton sofa for Stark, above, was inspired by mid-twentieth century design, and fits easily in a more contemporary room. The cut-outs in the back and arms have been carefully upholstered around the edges. I feel this piece is transparent enough to float in a room.

The tailored room should be lean, elegant, and modern, yet comfortable enough to be used for any occasion. Therefore, I opt for a monochromatic color scheme (instead of bright, zingy colors) deepened by exotic materials and carefully chosen spots of color. For inspiration, I look at 1970s designers who expertly combined materials—metal, rattan, and glass—for graphic effect. Furnishings should include clean-lined upholstery from the glamorous Art Deco period, to the more restrained Scandinavian styles of the 1950s and 1960s. I like to include side tables made from Lucite, glass, and metal, and carpets that are as simple as sisal or sometimes a bit flashier, like a silk-wool design emblazoned with geometric graphics. The architecture of the room should be minimal and spare. Instead of baroque moldings and arches, I prefer simple wood trim. Finally, it's important that the style of the light sources be just right. Skip the antiques; there are dozens of fantastic mid-century lighting designs, including sculptural pendants, chandeliers, floor lamps, and sconces available on the market.

LEFT In the foyer of a renovated house in Old Westbury, New York, Sherrill upholstered a sculptural Lucite bench in a traditional cut velvet. To similar effect, a vivid zebra-print carpet from Stark offsets the wall-covering panels made from earthy, woven straw. The photograph is of Le phénomène de l'extase, a 2005 work after Salvador Dalí, by Brazilian-born, New York-based artist Vik Muniz.

OPPOSITE Renovation updated the adjoining living room's traditional architecture. "I stripped away the moldings and added contemporary hardware to the windows and doors," explains the designer. The furniture includes a 1960s table and swivel tub chairs upholstered in cream-colored leather from Edelman. The window seat is dressed with pillows in lamb's wool, linen, and brown patent leather.

The den is one room where I like to turn up the fun. Lively colors, modern shapes, and whimsical accessories are combined to create an exciting space that sparks animated conversation and makes the den the most-used room in the house. Less formal than the living room—and usually more trafficked—the modern den is a place to experiment with a more daring range of colors. To create a feeling of excitement while maintaining the room's cozy, comfortable vibe, I chose earthy tones and turned them up a couple of notches: Instead of brick red, I used scarlet; instead of forest green, emerald. Accents of black and white and materials such as lacquer, linen, and shagreen contribute to the richness of the graphic effect. Usually, I hide the television in a cabinet and install shelves for art books and mementos. Also, I like to keep the lighting low. A modern pendant lamp will tie the room together and cast a warm glow. An overscale painting or a dramatic sculpture can push the room to another level.

RIGHT In a den on Long Island, the bright emerald green lacquered walls give the room an energetic lift. Covered in white patent leather, the tufted ottoman assumes a sculptural quality, while shaggy wool pillows, cut-velvet upholstery, a Lucite side table, and string-shade curtains create textural diversity. Graphic patterns appear, too, with the black-and-white prints on the armchairs and the contrasting piping on the sofa. "I went all out in this room," Sherrill admits. The sculpture is *The Multiplier's Vision #1*, 2007, by Halsey Rodman, from the Guild & Greyshkul gallery in New York.

NEW YORK
THE PLAZA

Wednesday 15 March 2006

Few things conjure up ideas of the excitement of urban glamour like New York's Plaza hotel. Built in 1900, it was designed by architect Henry Hardenbergh and modeled after a French chateau. Even today, the formal exterior looks like it should be filled with rooms done in a fussy, Old World decor. Although the acres of marble, dozens of crystal chandeliers, layers of baroque moldings, and famously ornate lobby still radiate Belle Epoque elegance, the recent addition of privately owned pieds-à-terre—in addition to the revamped hotel rooms—have changed the rules of decorating in this New York institution.

OPPOSITE In the media room of a pied-à-terre at the Plaza, a breakfast cup and saucer from Hermès sit on top of the March 15, 2006, Sotheby's auction catalog of objects from the hotel, which was renovated that year. The side table, with a natural agate stone top, is paired with an armchair covered in a preppy herringbone print from Holland & Sherry, an English company that specializes in traditional fabrics.

RIGHT Sherrill based the design of this room on the luxurious, streamlined spaces by 1940s French designer Jean-Michel Frank. Here the walls are upholstered in ivory leather from Edelman, and trimmed in a grid of mahogany wood. The painting of book jackets is by Canadian artist Paul Béliveau, from the Stricoff Fine Art gallery in New York. The custom upholstery is by De Angelis, New York; the carpet, from Edward Fields; and the brass floor lamp, by Cedric Hartman.

LEFT In a country house on Long Island, Sherrill set up a small seating area in the client's home office by using a pair of tufted club chairs. The Ultrasuede upholstery is a subdued contrast to the room's glossier elements, including the Elitis wallpaper, which mimics buffed cowhide, and a zebrawood coffee table designed by Sherrill. The spiral-shaped sculpture entitled *Turner Box* is a 2005 work by artist Marco Maggi from the Josée Bienvenu gallery in New York.

BELOW LEFT With its tidy palette of royal blue and white, a pair of floor lamps—with bases wrapped in shagreen from Sentimento in New York, and silk drum shades from B.B. Shades—frames a custom-made De Angelis sofa. The pillows, from Holland & Sherry, are in a geometric print made from applied felt, a motif repeated on the leather ottoman edged in a Greek-key pattern.

OPPOSITE This veranda in Palm Beach, Florida, was inspired by Sherrill's Hope Diamond fabric for Old World Weavers. The designer used it on all the upholstery, reversing it to show a white ground on a black background. The indoor-outdoor fabric is durable and the effect, Sherrill says, is "graphic and kicky."

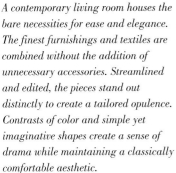

A contemporary living room houses the bare necessities for ease and elegance. The finest furnishings and textiles are combined without the addition of unnecessary accessories. Streamlined and edited, the pieces stand out distinctly to create a tailored opulence. Contrasts of color and simple yet imaginative shapes create a sense of drama while maintaining a classically comfortable aesthetic.

ABOVE In a New York apartment, a Biedermeier chest of drawers from Iliad Antiques in New York is paired with contemporary accessories, including a lamp with an agate base and an eighteenth-century Dutch mirror from Lee Calicchio in New York. Edward Fields custom-made the graphic blue-and-white silk carpet.

ABOVE Sherrill's clients use this antique chest to store collections of objects and silverware. "Any space looks so much sleeker when you keep clutter—even if it's 'artful'—to a minimum," the designer advises. With an antique églomisé mirror and a lamp made from a Chinese Export porcelain vase, the vignette set up in this foyer allows guests "a chance to reapply their lipstick before entering the main event," Sherrill adds.

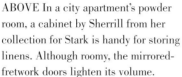

ABOVE In a city apartment's powder room, a cabinet by Sherrill from her collection for Stark is handy for storing linens. Although roomy, the mirrored-fretwork doors lighten its volume.

ABOVE Another cabinet, also by Sherrill, can be used as a media unit to store the television, along with its tangle of unsightly wires. Topped with a display of blue-and-white Chinese Export porcelain, the beveled-mirror doors, says the designer, "allow both the piece and the space to feel brighter and lighter."

OVERLEAF In an apartment at the Plaza, an eighteenth-century baroque mantelpiece is the focus of the living room, where modernist pieces are interspersed with elements of the past. A round, channel-back De Angelis sofa, covered in an ivory chenille from Scalamandré, and a collection of Chinese Export porcelain vases are in keeping with the blue-and-white color scheme. So is the painting by Isabel Bigelow, who is represented by the Sears-Peyton Gallery in New York. To create a more finished but not overdone space, plaster moldings were applied to the walls. The embroidery on the large pillow on the sofa was taken from the design in the custom-made carpet by Edward Fields in New York.

RIGHT When she was invited to participate in the 2006 Kips Bay Showhouse in New York, Sherrill created "The Lounge." She recalls that it "was an exciting room done in malachite, black, and white. The emerald green of the walls was produced by applying a mahogany glaze over the bright green color. This room was all about contrast and urban glamour. It felt like a sophisticated New York City playroom." The Ellipse wool rug is from the Sherrill Canet Collection for Stark, as are the brass and glass Sophia coffee tables and the Brighton étagère. The custom-made ottoman has been upholstered in a fabric from Old World Weavers. Sherrill also designed the zebra-hide, nail-studded framed mirror.

When streamlined decor starts to feel cold, I often incorporate something Asian to infuse it with texture and depth. The traditional colors of China—gold, red, and black—are wonderful to use and never feel dated.

OPPOSITE In a spacious Long Island living room with a soft color range of honeys and golds, a French Moderne settee sets the tone. The floor lamps with sculptural metal bases are from Fine Art Light; the pale-hued carpet is an antique Oriental.

ABOVE LEFT Adorned with tortoiseshell, a side chair with an angular fretwork back brings a textural touch of the past to the room's contemporary decor.

ABOVE Inspired by the tortoiseshell surface of the chair, Sherrill upholstered an ottoman in a leopard-patterned silk-velvet textile from Stark. "Animal prints work anywhere," she says. "In a velvet, they feel very exotic and luxurious, and play well with the Asian touches in the room."

LEFT In the living room, Sherrill used scale, not color, to create drama, teaming a tall eighteenth-century mirror with 1940s three-armed sconces by Jean Karajian, and a large glass coffee table. "For this room, I wanted to create a quiet, 'nothing unnecessary' approach," Sherrill explains. "Each piece of furniture has a connection to the next, which gives the room a seamless quality."

OPPOSITE A contemporary bronze mirror of twisted branches by the Paris-based designer Hervé van der Straeten, from Maison Gerard in New York, hangs above a custom-made leather console designed by Sherrill. The salmon-colored pillow, with its pattern of appliquéd velvet by Carol Davis, provides a dramatic single shot of color. The simple linen drapes are from Nobilis.

Because of their active lifestyles—which often include children and dogs running around the house—many of my clients require furnishings covered in textiles durable enough to last through the years. This need for high-performance fabrics speaks to a growing trend I like to call "the luxury of low maintenance." Thanks to innovations in textile technology, more companies than ever are creating tough fabrics that are as stunningly beautiful and as soft to the hand as they are tough and long-lasting. Also, the time and money spent on maintenance can be reduced with a few simple tricks: In addition to tech-savvy and machine-washable fabrics that can be made into slipcovers, choose dark, patterned carpets and surfaces that won't smudge, like rustic wood or honed marble.

RIGHT Filled with family and guests all summer long, nothing could be too delicate in this beach house on Eastern Long Island. The love seats in the large open living room are upholstered in an outdoor fabric from Sunbrella, as are the club chairs, done in a playful mix of plaids and stripes. The plaid, cotton-rag rug from Stark will also hold up to the traffic of sandy feet and dog paws. A textile piece by artist Sally Shore, woven of navy and white ribbon, conceals the television above the mantelpiece.

LEFT AND OPPOSITE In contrast to the interior architecture of the living room, where soft arches round out the space, the design of the kitchen features a geometric configuration of ceiling beams and wainscot designed by the architect Stuart Disston. The large space's slight variation in palette shows quieter shades of blue, edging out the vivid royal tone that runs through the rest of the house. Sherrill chose a deeper smoky blue for the island to make it stand out from the rest of the kitchen, including the paler blue cabinets. Natural wood edging, chosen to resemble driftwood, outlines the island to incorporate an organic element in the space. The industrial-style pendant fixtures are from Remains in New York.

This fabulous kitchen in Palm Beach was modeled after the Black Knight, my client's favorite vintage yacht. The room is completely outfitted in mahogany and black-painted wood to recall the boat's distinctive coloration.

OPPOSITE AND RIGHT An ornate crystal chandelier is at the entrance to this large, entertaining kitchen. Leaded glass doors can be pulled shut to separate the work area from the dining area. The custom-made dining tables can telescope from dining to cocktail height, depending on how the space is used. A banquette the length of the room was installed to accommodate large gatherings. Sherrill's Bel Aire chairs for Stark are on casters to swivel for easy television viewing and lively conversation. Sherrill also designed the Knight stools especially for this installation.

These days, the formal dining room has all but disappeared from many modern homes, having been absorbed by the kitchen or living room. I personally love a formal dining room, or at least a dining area that feels like a special space in its own right. Even if the dining room is little more than a breakfast nook, I challenge myself to make it into a main attraction by using combinations of colors, patterns, and styles that sometimes push the envelope and break the rules. The first question I ask is, "How many people should the dining room accommodate?" Also, "Can the table be made larger for a crowd?" And I insist that a table for serving be incorporated as a buffet. Then, after these decisions are made, it's time to mix up the styles of the furnishings and have some fun. I always choose a set of modern dining chairs, a wild, sculptural pair of table lamps, and an amazing mid-century hanging lamp or chandelier to tie everything together. Sometimes I'll come across an outstanding table, and since that is the raison d'être of a dining room, I'll design the rest of the room around it. A more formal dining area should have a carpet, whereas a breakfast nook might not; it all depends on how cozy you want the space to feel. Use curtains to help control the light and add an extra layer of color or pattern.

OPPOSITE AND RIGHT In the dining area of a New York apartment, Sherrill had the walls upholstered in navy blue striéd velvet from Scalamandré so that the trim pops and the walls keep things cozy, she says. Klismos-style chairs from De Angelis are covered in white leather to stand out against the dark blue background, like the custom-made Edward Fields carpet. The nineteenth-century French Regency table, from Lee Calicchio in New York, is elegant, as is the 1930s bronze Art Deco chandelier from Jean Karajian. An eighteenth-century painted Japanese screen from Naga Antiques hangs over the 1920s rosewood sideboard.

OPPOSITE AND ABOVE Beneath a lemon yellow
ceiling, nearly every surface in this Southampton,
New York, dining room sports a chocolate-and-white
pattern. Graphic patterns—on Sherrill's Parterre
carpet for Stark, her Caning wallpaper for Old World
Weavers, the mirror framed in zebra fabric, and the
ribbon panels by artist Sally Shore—create a lively
interior. "What makes this saturated use of pattern
work," Sherrill explains, "is the three-color palette,
which is consistent throughout, and the combinations
of different scales." The Duncan chairs, also
designed by Sherrill for Stark, and the 1970s dining
table from John Salibello Antiques in New York and
Bridgehampton, New York, are suitably animated.

OPPOSITE The dining area in this Long Island house is, Sherrill says, "spunky and graphic, as I mixed many periods and styles in a sophisticated, tasteful blend." A 1960s beige-linen–covered table by Karl Springer, a designer of luxurious furniture who often combined traditional shapes and exotic materials, has been paired with classic Chinese bamboo chairs.

RIGHT French 1930s table lamps with sculpted wood bases and peacock blue drum shades stand on a Parsons serving table. The large antique urns are from Morocco.

No matter how sleek the decor of a home, I always incorporate a few traditional designs into the bedroom to keep it soft. If I have an antique headboard, I like to add punchy graphic elements and bright colors to make the room feel young and fresh. The color scheme can be approached in a similar way. I have clients who prefer heavy shades in masculine hues like chocolate and dark red, to which I add bright white accents. For clients who prefer traditional bedroom decor but still want a contemporary look, I build a saturated palette of two contrasting colors: The tempo they create infuses the space with a modern dynamic.

OPPOSITE Sherrill designed the window treatments with a box pleat, and added royal blue trim to the drapes as a nod to the bed's pelmet. Situated by the window, the master bedroom's seating area is outfitted with club chairs in a velvet pinstripe from Ralph Lauren. Old-fashioned and contemporary styles are juxtaposed with accessories like monogrammed pillows, brass swing-lighting fixtures, ginger jars, and a carved mahogany and brass floor lamp. The carpet is a sisal from Stark.

RIGHT Saturated in royal blue and white, this New York City master bedroom's traditional style becomes bold, dramatic, and new. "This is one of my favorite examples of how to update a room by subtracting color until all that is left is one bold shade paired with the brightest white." A tailored, box-pleated pelmet crowns the headboard, which is upholstered in royal blue velvet and nailhead studs. Around this dramatic centerpiece, liberally applied textural patterns and shapes include tapestry pillows, ginger jars, and lamps with twisted mahogany bases.

ABOVE A twentieth-century starburst-shaped mirror in a gilded finish has been hung over a rosewood bed, from Sherrill Canet Interiors' Havana collection, that has been upholstered in a royal blue velvet. The mid-twentieth-century nightstands are topped with Lucite lamps from John Salibello Antiques. The bench at the foot of the bed is upholstered in a geometric-patterned cut velvet. Accessorizing the simple white quilt are custom-embroidered pillows by Carol Davis, and a cashmere throw.

ABOVE Crisp white bed linens bordered in dark red give a contemporary look to a barley-twist bed from Julia Gray. For her client, who likes to read in bed, Sherrill installed an extra-long picture light over a painting by Jackie Watson that was commissioned for the room. The nightstands are topped with figurines and lamps made of blue-and-white Chinese Export porcelain ginger jars from Ralph Lauren.

LEFT Lavish blue damask curtains from Watts of Westminster and an embroidered velvet pillow from Carol Davis contrast with the serene look of an ivory mohair-covered club chair in this master bedroom set in a city home. The navy blue piping is a crisp tailored detail.

OPPOSITE For this spacious sitting area in a master bedroom on Long Island, Sherrill upholstered a sofa from Kravet in a rich purple Ultrasuede from Robert Allen. "When you pair purple with gray and white, it feels so moody and modern," Sherrill says. The curtains, cornice, and delicate sheers from Corragio allow light to be filtered into the room. The pouf and bolster are upholstered in a gray-and-white zebra print from Clarence House. The patterned wool carpet is from Stark.

Abbott, James Archer. *Jansen*. New York: Acanthus Press, 2006.

Baldwin, Billy. *Billy Baldwin Decorates: A Book of Practical Decorating Ideas*. New York: Holt, Rinehart and Winston, 1972.

Baldwin, Billy. *Billy Baldwin Remembers*. New York: Harcourt Brace Javonovich, 1974.

Bartlett, Apple Parish and Susan Bartlett Crater. *Sister: The Life of Legendary American Interior Designer Mrs. Henry Parish*. New York: St. Martin's Press, 2000.

Cornforth, John. *English Interiors 1790-1848: The Quest for Comfort*. London: Barrie & Jenkins, 1978.

Dampierre, Florence de. *The Best of Painted Furniture*. New York: Rizzoli, 1987.

Domestic Architecture By H.T. Lindeberg. New York: William Helburn, 1940.

Forrest, Tim. *The Bulfinch Anatomy of Antique Furniture: An Illustrated Guide to Identifying Period, Detail, And Design*. London: Marshall Editions, 1996.

Hicks, Ashley. *David Hicks: A Life of Design*. New York: Rizzoli, 2009.

Hicks, David with Nicholas Jenkins. *Living With Design*. New York: William Morrow and Company, Inc., 1979.

Lewis, Adam. *Albert Hadley: The Story of America's Preeminent Interior Designer*. New York: Rizzoli, 2004.

Mackay, Robert B., Anthony K. Baker, and Carol A. Taylor (editors). *Long Island Country Houses And Their Architects, 1860-1940*. New York: W.W. Norton & Company, in association with the Society for the Preservation of Long Island Antiquities, 1997.

Martin-Vivier, Pierre-Emmanuel. *Jean-Michel Frank: L'étrange Luxe Du Rien*. Paris: Editions Norma, 2006.

Miller, Judith and Martin. *Period Style*. London: Mitchell Beazley, 1989.

Parish, Sister, Albert Hadley, and Christopher Petkanas. *Parish-Hadley: Sixty Years of Design*. Boston: Little, Brown and Company, 1995.

Secord, William. *Dog Painting 1840-1940: A Social History of the Dog in Art*. Suffolk: Antique Collectors' Club, 1992.

Spencer-Churchill, Henrietta. *Classic Decorative Details*. New York: Rizzoli, 1994.

Ypma, Herbert. *Paris Flea Market*. New York: Stewart, Tabori & Chang, 1996.

Unless noted, all images are either from the archives of Sherrill Canet Interiors, photographed by Michel Arnaud on location, or shot at the offices of Pointed Leaf Press by Pawel Kaminski. Any omissions will be corrected in future printings.

4: Jacques Malignon; 10: William Waldron; 14: Old Westbury Gardens, Richard Cheek photo, 1980; 16-17: Time & Life Pictures/Getty Images; 23: Time & Life Pictures/Getty Images; 24: Courtesy of Acanthus Press; 25: William Waldron; 27: William Waldron; 30-31: Courtesy of Acanthus Press; denniskrukowski.com; www.timleephoto.com; Tria Giovan tria@triagiovan.com; Courtesy of Albert Hadley; William Waldron; 32: ©marchphoto.com; 33: William Waldron; 34: Tria Giovan tria@triagiovan.com; 38: ©march-photo.com; 39: William Waldron; 44: William Waldron; 46: Courtesy of Acanthus Press; 48: ©marchphoto.com; 49: William Waldron; 52: ©marchphoto.com; 53: William Waldron; Tria Giovan tria@triagiovan.com; 54: William Waldron; Tria Giovan tria@triagiovan.com; 56: Courtesy of Acanthus Press; Tria Giovan tria@triagiovan.com; 60: Courtesy of Acanthus Press; 61: ©marchphoto.com; 64: Courtesy of Kentshire Galleries, New York; From *English Interiors 1790-1848: The Quest for Comfort* by John Cornforth, Barrie & Jenkins Ltd, 1978; Courtesy of Mario Buatta; 65: www.timleephoto.com; Copyright © Judith Miller and Dorling Kindersley Limited 2005; 66: Courtesy of Acanthus Press; 72-73: Tria Giovan tria@triagiovan.com; 74-75: Durston Saylor; 81: Durston Saylor; 84: Tria Giovan tria@triagiovan.com; 94: Durston Saylor; 106: From Billy Baldwin Decorates by Billy Baldwin, Holt McDougal, 1973; From *Over The Top: Helena Rubinstein: Extraordinary Style Beauty Art Fashion Design* by Suzanne Slesin, Pointed Leaf Press, 2003; Tria Giovan tria@triagiovan.com; William Waldron; 107: Photograph by Rene and Barbara Stoeltie, from *Paris Flea Market* by Herbert Ypma, Harry N. Abrams, Inc. 1996; Francis Smith; 112-113: Francis Smith; 119: Tria Giovan tria@triagiovan.com; 128: Durston Saylor; 134-135: From *In The Pink: Dorothy Draper, America's Most Fabulous Decorator*, Pointed Leaf Press, 2006; www.timleephoto.com; The Estate of David Hicks; Art et Industrie/©Éditions Norma, Paris; 140: William Waldron; 143: Robin Roslund, Arne Roslund Photography; 148-149: www.timleephoto.com; 154-157: John M. Hall Photographs; 158-159: Robin Roslund, Arne Roslund Photography; 162-163: Anastassios Mentis; 166-167: Tria Giovan tria@triagiovan.com

SIDE/NESTING/NIGHT TABLES

AMAZON SIDE TABLE
18" W x 22" D x 18" H
Gilded natural wood with glass top. (Custom finishes available)

MONROE NIGHT TABLE
30" W x 20" D x 26" H
Paper parchment. (Also available in goat skin parchment and lacquer)

PAVILLION NESTING TABLE
23.5" W x 14" D x 22" H
Lacquer. (Also available in goat skin parchment, paper parchment)

ST. PETERSBURG SIDE TABLE
30" W x 30" D x 29" H
Walnut wood top, ebony wood curved base, rosewood base, brass gilded ball feet.

PRADO TABLE
24" W x 24" D x 16" H
Dark zebra wood top, and base. Brass band detail around top and edge of the base.

TABOURETTE SIDE TABLE
15" Dia x 19" H
Leather wrapped body. Brass binding with brass nailheads. Milk glass top. Brass ball feet.

COCKTAIL/COFFEE/CONSOLE TABLES

ARABESQUE COFFEE TABLE
54" W x 20" D x 16" H
Brass frame with 3/8" glass top. (Custom finishes available)

BRIDGEHAMPTON NESTING COFFEE TABLE
48" W x 36" D x 17" H
Paper parchment. (Also available in goat skin parchment and lacquer)

CARLTON COCKTAIL TABLE
48" W x 32" D x 15" H
Brass frame. Transparent glass top and shelf. (Custom finishes available)

EDUARDO COFFEE TABLE
48" W x 36" D x 18" H
Dark zebra wood top and side frame. Rosewood legs, brass feet, glass top.

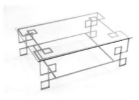

LINLEY CONSOLE TABLE
65" W x 20" D x 35" H
Ivory crocodile embossed leather covered top and base, 1" brass rod with brass finials.

RIDGEWAY CONSOLE
60" W x 18" D x 34" H
Bone. (Custom finishes available)

SOPHIA COFFEE TABLE
48" W x 24" D x 18" H
Brass frame with transparent glass top. (Custom finishes available)

BENCH

CARLTON BENCH
30" W x 19" D x 18" H
Brass frame with upholstered cushion. (Custom finishes available)

DESKS

ANTOINETTE DESK
60" W x 30" D x 30" H
Black lacquer with ivory leather tooled top. Custom brass hardware. (Custom finishes available)

SLOANE DESK
60" W x 22" D x 30" H
Bleached maple. (Custom finishes available)

CHEST/ARMOIRE/ETAGERE

ASHLEY CHEST OF DRAWERS
60" W x 20" D x 34" H
Bleached maple wood with brass inlays. Custom brass hardware. (Custom finishes available)

BRIGHTON ETAGERE
40" W x 18" D x 86" H
Brass frame. Bronze joints, top and feet details. Glass shelves, no bevel. (Custom finishes available)

PAVILLION ARMOIRE
45" W x 23" D x 83" H
Black lacquer with custom brass pulls. (Custom finishes available)

SCREEN
3 PANEL SCREEN
90" W x 84" H
Fully upholstered, brass nailheads
front and back, Brass hinges.

DINING CHAIRS
EATON ARMED DINING CHAIR
24" W x 18" SH x 18" SD x
24" AH x 39" H
Mahogany, dark brown legs,
upholstered.

DUCAN DINING CHAIR
22" D x 20" SW x 20" SD x 38.5" H
Mahogany, dark brown legs,
upholstered.

ARM/CLUB CHAIRS
BEL AIRE CHAIR
31" W x 28" D x 30" H
Mahogany, dark brown legs,
upholstered.

BELLE HAVEN CLUB CHAIR
31" W x 36" D x 24" SD x 33" H
Mahogany, dark brown legs,
upholstered.

BRINDALLE CHAIR
31.5" W x 29" D x 35" H
Mahogany, dark brown legs,
upholstered.

CARNEGIE CLUB CHAIR
30" W x 36" D x 24" AH x 34" H
Fully upholstered.

ELIZABETH CHAIR
33" W x 40" D x 22" SD x 32" H
Mahogany, dark brown legs,
upholstered.

KENSINGTON CLUB CHAIR
30" W x 34" D x 36" H
Mahogany, dark brown legs,
upholstered.

PIMLICO WING CHAIR
30" W x 22" SD x 25" AH x 40" H
Mahogany, dark brown legs,
upholstered.

SOFAS
EATON SOFA
82" W x 32" D x 31" H
Mahogany, dark brown legs,
upholstered.

ELIZABETH SOFA
78" W x 36" D x 31" H
Mahogany, dark brown legs,
upholstered.

GREENWICH SOFA
82" W x 38" D x 28" SD x 34" H
Fully upholstered.

HEMINGWAY DAYBED
70.5" W x 32" D x 25.5" H
Mahogany, dark brown legs,
upholstered.

HEMINGWAY SOFA
84" W x 38" D x 34" H
Mahogany, dark brown legs,
upholstered.

JORDAN CHAISE WITH
BOLSTER
72" W x 30" D x 19" SH x 32" H
Mahogany, dark brown legs,
upholstered.

KNOLE SOFA
80 1/2" W x 36" D x 35" H
Fully upholstered.

OTTOMAN
BALZAC OTTOMAN
27.75" W x 27.75" D x 17.50" H
Gold leaf feet and platform,
upholstered cushions. (Also
available in silver leaf or lacquer)

THIS BOOK IS DEDICATED TO MY WONDERFUL FAMILY

To my husband Eduardo and my children Eduardo and Alejandro. They have given me unending support as a working mother and wife with great sacrifices throughout my career. I also thank my mother for being my biggest cheerleader. And many thanks to my dearest friends who have always been a source of strength and inspiration; they are always there when I need a shoulder or a laugh.

A special thanks to the fabulously creative Suzanne Slesin and her team, including Regan Toews and Jonathan Lazzara at Pointed Leaf Press. Suzy took a body of work and gave it a framework, definition, and meaning. Thank you to Stafford Cliff who, working with Dominick J. Santise Jr., designed the layout of the book with great success. Damaris Colhoun turned my thoughts into words that describe two decades. Also, Michel Arnaud should be celebrated for his ability to capture the essence of a room in a single frame.

I am beyond grateful to my talented and loyal staff. Christina Danka, Irina Maslij in the New York office, and Claire Poulikidis and Kathy Siegel in Locust Valley. Together we manage to keep clients happy and create wonderful spaces. We even manage to have some fun during what is generally a frantic pace. I depend on them and truly appreciate their hard work and dedication over the years. Thank you, thank you, thank you.

Thank you to Mary S. Phipps who took the time to reflect on life on the North Shore of Long Island and how it is truly a special place to live, and sharing this with us for all to enjoy and appreciate.

Thank you to Robert Israel of Kentshire Galleries who embodies the importance of preserving the past in his appreciation and expertise in procuring fabulous antique furnishings. Without his firm, designers and their projects would not shine as brightly.

The Stark family has given me a wonderful opportunity to showcase my designs in mediums from rugs, fabric and wallcoverings and now with a collection of furniture. A special thank you to John Stark, Steven Stark, Ashley Stark and Rick Zolt for committing to an aesthetic that we all found pleasing. Also, thank you to the entire staff at Stark and Old World Weavers for their continued support and encouragement.

A special thank you to the many talented architects that I have been honored to work with over the years. Without incredible architectural details and teamwork, these projects would not be the same. Also, thank you to the many editors who have been supportive of my work and the writers and photographers who captured the designs. Without our favorite artisans, vendors, workrooms, craftsmen and contractors we would not be able to produce what at times verged on the impossible, including: GBC Upholstery, DeAngelis Upholstery, Fabrizi Custom Furniture, New Day Woodwork, Window Modes, Mark Skinner Interiors, Interiors by J.C. Landa, Hokanson, Edward Fields, Duce Construction, The Mayfair Group, Qualico Construction, Iliad, Kentshire, Florian Papp, and countless others—thank you.

My clients are my biggest inspiration to creative design and I thank you all for giving me the opportunity to hopefully realize the dream of living well, beautifully.—SHERRILL CANET, New York, July 2010

CAPTIONS

FRONT COVER Motif, a silk fabric shown in its Espresso colorway, is one of Sherrill Canet's designs for Old World Weavers.

BACK COVER A mirror by the designer Hervé van der Straeten, from Maison Gerard in New York, stars in a Gold Coast living room by Sherrill Canet Interiors.

FRONT ENDPAPERS LEFT In a royal blue and white media room at the Plaza hotel, the walls are upholstered in leather and trimmed in a grid of mahogany wood.

FRONT ENDPAPERS RIGHT Sherrill added a pillow made from a rare antique textile as a counterpoint to the sofa's graphic silk stripes in a formal living room on Long Island.

BACK ENDPAPERS Spyra is a Sherrill Canet Collection fabric for Old World Weavers.

HALF TITLE Sherrill Canet's Ellipse carpet was her first design produced by Stark. It made its debut at the Kips Bay Designer Showhouse in New York in 2006 to rave reviews and is now available in four colorways.

TITLE PAGE From the architect's floor plans, Sherrill Canet Interiors creates furniture placement schemes.

CONTENTS In 2010, Sherrill was photographed in the library of her house in Locust Valley, New York.

PAGE 28 In the late 1980s, the Canets moved to a Long Island house by Harrie T. Linderberg.

PAGE 29 Caning, in its Grass colorway, is a Sunbrella indoor-outdoor fabric from one of Sherrill Canet collections for Old World Weavers.

PAGE 62 A Long Island house designed by Oliver Cope of Oliver Cope Architect was inspired by traditional French and English country manors.

Page 63 Interlochen, shown here in the Strawberry Ganache colorway, is part of a collection Sherrill designed for Old World Weavers in 2009.

PAGE 104 With its graceful arched double doors and low-hanging roof, this Long Island house by Stuart Disston of Austin Patterson Disston Architects recalls the timeless appeal of French country manses.

PAGE 105 Robin's Egg is one of the color choices of Filigree, a Sunbrella fabric collection Sherrill designed for Old World Weavers.

PAGE 132 Designed by architect Harry Hardenbergh, the Plaza hotel was built in 1900, with a grand façade that was modeled after a medieval French chateau.

PAGE 133 Time Squared, one of Sherrill's designs for Old World Weavers, is shown in its ivory colorway.

Pointed Leaf Press would like to thank: Mario Buatta, Barry Cenower of Acanthus Press, Marion D.S. Dreyfus, Elizabeth Gall, Pawel Kaminski, Deanna Kawitzky, Tony Manning, and Monica Randall.

SHERRILL CANET INTERIORS, LTD.
3 East 66th Street, Suite 4B
New York, NY 10065
T: (212) 396-1194
Fax: (212) 396-1294
www. sherrillcanet.com

POINTED LEAF PRESS, LLC.
136 Baxter Street
New York, NY 10013
www.pointedleafpress.com

Printed and bound in China

First edition
10 9 8 7 6 5 4 3 2 1
Library of Congress Control Number: 2010928599
ISBN 10: 0-9823585-4-7
ISBN 13: 978-0-9823585-4-2